The Contemporary Monologue

ridge *danyers*
Library

This book must be returned on or before the above date.
Fines will be charged on all overdue items.

by the same authors

The Contemporary Monologue (Men)
The Modern Monologue (Women and Men)
The Classical Monologue (Women and Men)
Soliloquy! The Shakespeare Monologues (Women and Men)
Solo: The Best Monologues of the 80s (Women and Men)

The
Contemporary Monologue
Women

Edited with notes and commentaries by

MICHAEL EARLEY
& PHILIPPA KEIL

Methuen Drama

First published in Great Britain 1995
by Methuen Drama
215 Vauxhall Bridge Road, London SW1V 1EJ

10 9 8

Methuen Publishing Limited Reg. No. 3543167

Copyright in the selections, format, introductions and commentaries
© 1995 Michael Earley and Philippa Keil

The editors have asserted their moral rights

ISBN 0–413–68110–6

A CIP catalogue record for this book
is available at the British Library

Papers used by Methuen Publishing Limited
are natural, recyclable products made from wood grown in
sustainable forests. The manufacturing processes conform to
the environmental regulations of the country of origin

Typeset by Wilmaset Ltd, Birkenhead, Wirral
Printed and bound in Great Britain by
Cox & Wyman Ltd, Reading, Berkshire

Front cover: Fiona Shaw
Photograph by Ivan Kyncl

Contents

Notes to the Actor

The monologues in this volume come from plays produced and published in Britain and America over the past ten years. Each identifies some facet of contemporary thought and feeling. They augment the speeches in our two previous volumes, *The Modern Monologue* and *The Classical Monologue*, as well as supplement and update a volume we published a number of years ago, *Solo: The Best Monologues of the 80s*. Our aim in all these books has been to provide actors with the kind of material that holds the stage and challenges the performer to use skills that will show her to best advantage.

When we put these volumes together we deliberately choose speeches from plays that are in print and readily available. (See *Play Sources* at the end of this volume.) You simply must read the whole play for the fullest context of any speech. A monologue can never be the whole story of a particular drama. It is always just one character's point of view at an isolated moment in the action. One story linked to many others. As an actor, you cannot possibly glean all that is relevant about a character's life, likes and dislikes, behaviour, place in the plot or even why she speaks unless you have followed that character's progress through the entire play. You have to know the playwright's style and what he or she is attempting to say in these isolated moments and how to weigh it against other scenes and speeches. A collection of monologues like this can get an actor started but should take you back to the plays from which these speeches have been selected.

To help you begin your work on these pieces our Introductions summarize a play's action up to the point the speech begins. We have also tried to give you a brief sketch of the character that might be helpful, using where possible the playwright's own words. In the Commentary after each monologue we alert you to details in the speech that could help you to act it better. A warning though:

these are not director's notes, since our aim is not to dictate how these monologues should be performed. That's a job we must leave open to each individual performer. But any good dramatist includes notes of direction in the very rhythm and structure of speeches and dialogue. So what we have done in each Commentary is to put you on the trail of these vital stylistic clues so you can appreciate what the writer has given you to act. In most instances the path of a speech is self-evident and needs little gleaning. But since we work with actors on a daily basis, we know that even the smallest observations and hints about the language of a speech can help improve a performance: the repetition of a single word, an obsession with a prop, the way a character seems to be avoiding something unspoken, or the way she expresses a vital need are all the kinds of clues you can find in the character's choice of words.

What makes the monologues which follow so contemporary is their common currency and their ability to engage with life as we live it now. As contemporary events bear down on us playwrights respond to the crises and pressures in different ways. Practically all the speeches in this book are preoccupied with self-contradictions of one kind or another. Loneliness and sexual conflict, for example, are two themes which are repeated again and again. A character always speaks out in a play because she has something to say and must be heard. An actor has to listen to the character in order really to hear what she is saying. Perhaps the only and best bit of direction to leave you with when doing a monologue is to feel the need to speak, know what you are speaking about and to whom, and the words will connect with what you have to say.

Michael Earley
Philippa Keil
London 1995

After Easter
Anne Devlin

Scene 1. A hospital room somewhere in England.

Greta (37) was born in Northern Ireland. She now lives in Oxford with her husband and their three children (eleven-year-old twins and a new-born baby). Her academic husband is having an affair and Greta wants a divorce even though she knows she will not get custody of the children. She is a lapsed Catholic and has been having hallucinations; the apparitions always coincide with the Catholic feast days of Pentecost and Candlemas. She is also prone to depression and her behaviour has become increasingly unpredictable. Following an incident in which she was found sitting in the middle of a road after abruptly running away from a dinner party, her husband has had her institutionalized in a mental hospital. The incident was interpreted as an attempt at suicide. But for Greta it was a statement about her life, her husband's affair and her sense of alienation from her Irish roots and her religion. She is an exile from every aspect of her own life. She is experiencing a crisis of identity. She is burdened by the past but cannot escape it and repeatedly cries 'I don't want to be Irish'. In this speech, which opens the play, she begins to reveal her unusual personality to the audience as she sits cross-legged on the floor or on a bed.

GRETA. I have often found when you can't do anything else you can always sit on the road. It's better than screaming. It makes everyone else scream. It makes me very quiet. My mother used to scream. She'd run upstairs after me and pull my hair. I'd sit behind the bedroom door for hours – with the bed pushed up against it. And she'd scream and scream and pound the door. But she couldn't get in. Nobody could. After a while she'd stop and go downstairs. And she'd forget about it. Then I'd put my head down and go to sleep. She'd shout, 'Nobody loves you! Nobody loves you!' And I'd think it doesn't matter because I love me. I don't need anyone. And then I'd tickle myself, and that would make me smile. Until one day – there was a day we collected outside the university, it was a small march from the Students' Union. And just at the beginning as we linked up to start – I was in the front row, it was very peaceful – we linked arms and suddenly I had this rush of things, as if everything was suddenly centred in one place and it started to move, and it started to make me smile, and I kept trying not to smile; but the smile kept coming until I couldn't hold it back any longer and it grew and grew so big. And then we stepped forward and moved off.

I didn't go on any more marches after that. The rest of the day seemed very flat, it seemed to me – as if that was the point. And anyway lots of other things make me smile . . . the sun shining through the bedroom window on my cunt.

COMMENTARY: The speech is calculated to give Greta lots of focus and to concentrate our attention on her. The story and Greta's plight is so unusual that the words barely need dramatizing in order to have an effect. It's an excellent example of a monologue which forces the listener to come to you in order to hear what you say. The character just sits cross-legged on her bed, a spotlight on her face. The delivery is quite matter-of-fact and quiet. And yet the speech is also full of sound and commotion (other people 'screaming' and 'shouting'). The speech demands that you capture Greta's calm inner peace (which has a very spiritual quality) while remembering that she exists in a world which for her is devoid of both love and meaning.

Angels in America Part One: Millennium Approaches
Tony Kushner

Act 1, scene 3. Harper's apartment, Brooklyn. Autumn 1985. She is alone.

Harper Amaty Pitt (20s) is 'an agoraphobic with a mild valium addiction'. She is married to Joe, a clerk in the Court of Appeals. They are both Mormons from Salt Lake City. She rarely ventures out and her grasp of reality is shaky. The radio has become her main contact with the outside world, and she has become particularly sensitive to ecological issues and disasters. Her pill-popping causes her to hallucinate. She is not only isolated from the world but from her husband both emotionally and sexually. 'She is listening to the radio and talking to herself, as she often does. She speaks to the audience.'

HARPER. People who are lonely, people left alone, sit talking nonsense to the air, imagining . . . beautiful systems dying, old fixed orders spiralling apart . . .

When you look at the ozone layer, from outside, from a spaceship, it looks like a pale blue halo, a gentle, shimmering aureole encircling the atmosphere encircling the earth. Thirty miles above our heads, a thin layer of three-atom oxygen molecules, product of photosynthesis, which explains the fussy vegetable preference for visible light, its rejection of darker rays and emanations. Danger from without.

It's a kind of gift, from God, the crowning touch to the creation of the world: guardian angels, hands linked, make a spherical net, a blue-green nesting orb, a shell of safety for life itself. But everywhere, things are collapsing, lies surfacing, systems of defence giving way . . . This is why, Joe, this is why I shouldn't be left alone. (*Little pause.*)

3

I'd like to go travelling . . . Leave you behind to worry. I'll send postcards with strange stamps and tantalizing messages on the back. 'Later maybe.' 'Nevermore . . .'

COMMENTARY: Harper speaks in unconnected sentences that sound like nonsense. Harper just floats. But the effect she creates is that of someone having a vision. Like many of the characters in Kushner's play she is in touch with a fantasy world; a rootless wanderer searching for peace and contentment. Harper views life and experience through a haze. Her world is in a constant state of evolution and flux. The words she uses are a mixture of religion, science and psychobabble. She expresses a deep need for companionship, a fear of being alone and a sense of structures collapsing all around her. The final word she says is significant: 'nevermore'.

Assassins
Stephen Sondheim (music & lyrics)
and John Weidman (book)

Scene 6. A public park in America. 1975.

*Lynette 'Squeaky' Fromme (27) is a disciple of Charles Manson. She
has had an average middle-class childhood in the suburbs of Los
Angeles. She took ballet lessons as a child and was a cheerleader in high
school. In 1967, when she was nineteen, she met Charles Manson on
the beach in Venice, California. She became one of his disciples and a
member of the infamous Manson Family, which committed the brutal
Tate-LoBianca murders for which Manson was tried and imprisoned.
Fromme believes that Manson is the Messiah and that the world can
only be saved if his teachings are heeded. To this end, she decides to
commit a crime for which she will be arrested and at her trial she will
then call Manson as a witness so that he can use it as a forum to address
the world. In this scene, while high on marijuana, she describes how she
met Charlie.*

FROMME. I was like you once. Lost. Confused. A piece of
shit. (MOORE *nods philosophically*.) Then I met Charlie . . .
I was sitting on the beach in Venice. I'd just had a big fight
with my daddy about, I don't know, my eye make-up or the
bombing of Cambodia. He said I was a drug addict and a
whore and I should get out of his house forever–
[MOORE. I think there's a new perfume called Charlie.]
I went down to the beach and sat down on the sand and
cried. I felt like I was disappearing. Like the whole world
was dividing into two parts. Me, and everybody else. And
then this guy came down the beach, this dirty-looking little
elf. He stopped in front of me and smiled this twinkly devil
smile and said, 'Your daddy kicked you out.' He knew!

5

'Your daddy kicked you out!' How could he know? My daddy didn't tell him, so who could've? *God*. God sent this dirty-looking little elf to save a little girl lost on a beach. He smiled again and touched my hair and off he went. And for a minute I just watched him go. Then I ran and caught his hand, and till they arrested him for stabbing Sharon Tate, I never let it go.

COMMENTARY: Lynette sounds like a lost child with a high pitched voice which is probably why she has the nickname 'Squeaky'. The story has a wonderful simplicity, like one of those parables in the New Testament where Christ the Messiah meets a beggar along the side of the road. Someone awe-inspiring has entered Squeaky's life and now, though many years later, the moment is still strongly felt. On 5 September 1975 she aimed a loaded gun at President Gerald Ford as he left the Senator Hotel in Sacramento, California. As planned, she was arrested and tried, but Manson was not allowed to testify.

Belfry
Billy Roche

Act 1. The belfry of a Roman Catholic church in Wexford, a small town in Ireland.

Angela (late 30s) is married to Donal and has several children. Her husband works night shifts at the local factory and finds 'heaven' at the local handball alley. He is an extremely possessive husband. Angela cleans the local church and arranges the flowers. She is a gentle sympathetic woman. Her positive and optimistic spirit brings a new life into the male world of the church. She and the church sacristan, Artie O'Leary, find they share a compatible sensibility and become increasingly drawn to one another. They start as friends and become lovers, meeting secretly in the church belfry. Angela describes the impact of their relationship: 'I brought you back to life and you taught me to soar again and that's somethin' isn't it? I soared in your arms Artie.' Together they find a romantic escape from their lonely and humdrum lives. But for both of them this is untypical; Artie lives with his bedridden mother and has never had a girlfriend, let alone an affair, and Angela is a dutiful wife. In this scene she and Artie are together in the belfry, and she begins to reveal a different side of her character in this speech.

ANGELA. I went up to see my sister Maude this afternoon . . . I wanted to tell her all about yeh. But I couldn't. It's funny, there was a time when we used to tell each other everythin'. Until I discovered that I was doin' all the talkin'. We used to go nearly everywhere together – myself and Maude – off to all the dances and all. We were as mad as hatters, the pair of us. Well I was anyway! (*She chuckles.*)
[ARTIE. What?]
We joined the Irish dancin' one time. We used to come out onto the back of an auld lorry or somewhere and your man'd

7

start up on the accordion. Bum bum bum bum bum bum bum. Bum bum bum bum bum bum bum . . . All the boys'd gather round and try to look up our dresses. Meself and Maude used to give them a right eye full I can tell yeh. [ARTIE. Were yeh any good?

At What? Dancin'? No we weren't.] Sure we hardly ever practised or anythin'. I just wanted to get up and show off in front of the crowd like yeh know. I probably should have been a singer in a band or somethin' Artie shouldn't I? When we were young I was forever draggin' poor Maude down to stand outside the Town Hall every Friday night. It was durin' the Rock 'n Roll days and we could see them all jivin' inside – the boys in their snazzy suits, the girls in their big dresses and all. I used to be dyin' to go in there. I'd've loved that now – clackin' along in me high heel shoes . . . By the time we were old enough to go though the whole scene had started to change . . . Keep away from Padraic Lacy, me mother said to me when we were goin' off to our very first dance. Why? says I. Never mind why, says she. Just keep away from him that's all. Padraic Lacy had a car and there was a rumour goin' around that he had slipped a girl a Mickey Finn one night after a dance and while she was drowsy he put his hand up her skirt. He was one of the first boys I ever went out with. I thought he was a right creep. He started to cry when I told him I didn't want to see him again. Maude was lookin' for a prince or some sort of a sheik to whisk her off to God knows where. She was goin' out with this fella from Tuam who came to town to work in the bank. A real good lookin' fella with sultry eyes. Maude dropped him like a hot brick when she found out that his Da was a plasterer. She was a real snob. She married a guard in the end and went off to live in suburbia . . . I never really wanted all the things that other people seem to long for Artie yeh know. Maybe that's why I got them hah? . . . Donal is still down in the dumps over that auld handball match. The young fella ran rings around him I heard. He won't go out nor nothin' now. He just mopes around the house all day drinkin' mugs of tay. I think he feels it's an end of an era or somethin'. And maybe he's right . . .

COMMENTARY: The passing years have made Angela shy and secretive. Here, though, she reveals a time when the discovery and experiment of youth held attractions. She was bold and adventurous. The vividness of music and dance come through in the descriptions and suddenly the speech becomes very active as Angela is transported back to her rock'n'roll days; to a time of sensual and sexual awakening. Her words cascade forth in a wonderful rhythm that encapsulates key incidents of her youth. But notice how she slips back into her shell near the end of the speech. For the length of this monologue, however, Angela must seem like a fresher, younger and freer woman. It's Artie who takes her back to these moments.

Brontëburgers
Victoria Wood

The Haworth Parsonage, Yorkshire, North England.

Guide (20s-30s) works as the official tour guide to the Haworth Parsonage (family home to the Brontë sisters). She takes her job seriously but gives her tours a uniquely personal touch. She is a victim of the heritage industry. In fact, she reveals more about herself in this speech than she does about the Parsonage or the literary sisters; she even admits that she hasn't read any of their novels. Her frame of reference is entirely dictated by her suburban lifestyle and TV. This speech is a self-contained stand-up comedy monologue.

GUIDE. Right, I'm your official guide. Now before I show you round, I'll just fill you in on a few details, as we call them. As you can see, we're standing in the hall of the Haworth Parsonage, where Haworth's parson, the Reverend Brontë, lived here with his daughters, the famous Brontë sisters, now, alas, no longer with us – but they have left us their novels, which I've not read, being more of a Dick Francis nut. Now, if you pass by me into the parlour (mind my vaccination) . . . This is what was known in those days as a parlour, somewhat similar to our lounge-type sitting-room affair in modern terminology. I'm afraid the wallpaper isn't the original period to which we're referring to, it is actually Laura Ashley, but I think it does give some idea of what life must have been like in a blustery old Yorkshire community of long ago.

That portrait on the wall is actually of Charlotte Brontë, one of the famous Brontë sisters, and of course to us she may seem a rather gloomy-looking individual; but you must remember these days she'd have a perm, or blusher, or I suppose even drugs would have helped her maintain a more cheerful attitude. In fact, she'd probably not be dead if she was alive today. Now if you'd like to hutch through to the Reverend Brontë's study . . . This is a typical study in which to do studying – as you can see there's a table, chair . . . (oh my poncho, I've been looking for that . . .) and I like to imagine this elderly old gentleman hunched over a sermon, probably thinking, 'Where's my cocoa, I suppose those darn girls are in the middle of another chapter,' or something like that he may have been thinking – we just can't be sure . . . Of course he died eventually, unfortunately. You must remember this is an extremely exposed part of the United Kingdom, I mean, it's May now, and I'm still having to slip that polo-neck under my bolero.

On the table we see the Reverened Brontë's gloves. They tell us such a lot about him. He had two hands, and he wasn't missing any fingers. We think they were knitted by one of the famous Brontë sisters. I don't suppose their brother Branwell could knit and anyway being an alcoholic he'd never have been able to cast on.

Now if you'd just hutch up the stairs . . . We're looking out over the graves to the hills beyond. And, fairly clearly in the distance we can hear the wind 'wuthering'. That's an old Yorkshire word; some other old Yorkshire words are 'parkin' and 'fettle'. The room in which we're now standing in was originally Charlotte's mother's bedroom. In fact Charlotte's mother died in this room, and Charlotte died in here too, so better not stay too long! (Just my joke!) In that glass case you'll see what we call a day dress – that is a dress worn in the day, not at night – we think belonging to Anne or Emily, presumably not Branwell, unless he had more problems than history's prepared to tell us.

A few dates for the date-minded. The Brontë family moved here some time in the nineteenth century, and lived here for quite a number of years. As I say, Charlotte died in this room – those are her slippers. And I like to imagine her in this room, with her slippers on, dying.

Now if you go through the far door, yes, do move my moped . . . Now this room was at one time Branwell's room. I think people tend to forget Branwell was fairly artistic himself. Of course, he was lazy, conceited and a dipsomaniac, so these days he'd have probably been in the government.

Now if anybody would like a souvenir to take home as a souvenir, we have Brontë video-games, body-warmers, acrylic mitts, pedestal mats, feminine deodorants and novelty tea-strainers. Snacks and light refreshments are available in the Heathcliff Nosher Bar, so please feel free to sample our very popular Brontëburgers. Or for the fibre-conscious – our Branwell Brontëburgers.

Oh – just a little message for the 'Yorkshire Heritage' coach party. Can they please re-convene at two in the car-park ready for this afternoon's trip which is, I believe, round three dark Satanic mills, Emmerdale Farm, and Nora Batty's front room? Thank you.

COMMENTARY: The actor will stress the comedy best by creating a vivid character in the Guide. This is an illustrated lecture and you move the audience from place to place and must imagine yourself surrounded by a small party of tourists who appear to hang on your every word. The Guide constantly reveals how uncultured she is but feels no embarrassment about this. She could easily be taking groups through a model home on a newly built estate. She has no sense of place or history. But she certainly has a great sense of herself and her own opinions.

Burn This
Lanford Wilson

Act I. Anna's huge loft in a converted cast-iron building in lower Manhattan, New York City. The time is the present. Six o'clock in the evening, mid-October.

Anna (32) is a dancer and choreographer. She is 'very beautiful, tall and strong'. Her roommate and dance partner of twelve years, Robbie, has died in a freak boating accident with his gay lover. She and her new roommate, Larry, have been out to the mid-West to Robbie's funeral. Since Robbie's family did not realize he was gay, Anna plays the role of his girlfriend. The whole experience was a 'total nightmare' for her. The family were not interested in hearing about the real Robbie – the dancer and homosexual – and Anna had to maintain the lie for them. She has had three vodkas and her first cigarette since college days. She is tired and emotionally drained, and is not looking forward to her trip tomorrow to be with her dance company for a première in Texas. For the past two days she has worn the same clothes and has not exercised. At this point all she wants to do is take a hot bath. As she says 'I feel like a piece of shit, I'm not very good company.' Here she recounts to Larry what it was like spending the previous night with Robbie's family.

ANNA. [No,] I should have come with you. God. Just as I think I'm out of there, some relatives drive me back to the house. The place is mobbed. I'm dragged through everybody eating and drinking and talking, to some little back bedroom, with all the aunts and cousins, with the women, right? Squashed into this room. His mother's on the bed with a washcloth on her forehead. I'm trying to tell them how I've got to get a bus back to civilization.
[LARRY. This is very moving, but I'm double-parked.
ANNA. Exactly.
LARRY. This is a *wake*?]

13

I couldn't tell you *what* it was, Larry, I guess. In about eight seconds I know they have no idea that Robbie's gay.

[LARRY. I could have told you that.]

They've never heard of Dom. God, I'm making up stories, I'm racking my brain for every interesting thing anyone I know has done to tell them Robbie did it. Wonderful workaholic Robbie, and I couldn't tell them a thing about him. It was all just so massively sad.

[LARRY. Oh, Lord.]

It gets worse, it gets much worse. And they *never saw him dance*! I couldn't believe it. All the men are gorgeous, of course. They all look exactly like Robbie except in that kind of blue-collar, working-at-the-steel-mill kind of way, and *drink*? God, could they knock it back. So then it's midnight and the last bus has left at ten, which they knew, I'm sure, damn them, and I hadn't checked, like an idiot. So I have to spend the night in Robbie's little nephew's room in the attic. The little redhead, did you see him?

[LARRY. I didn't see him.]

He's been collecting butterflies all day, and they're pinned around the room to the walls – a pin in each wing, right?

[LARRY. I'm not liking this little redheaded nephew.]

Darling, wait. So. I get to sleep by about two, I've got them to promise to get me up at six-thirty for the seven-something bus. I wake up, it's not quite light, really; you can't see in the room much – but there's something *in* there.

[LARRY. Oh, God.]

There's this intermittent soft flutter sound. I think what the hell is – Larry, the – oh, Lord, the walls are just pulsating. All those butterflies are alive. They're all beating their bodies against the walls – all around me. The kid's put them in alcohol; he thought he'd killed them, they'd only passed out.

[LARRY. Oh, God.]

I started screaming hysterically. I got the bedsheet around me, ran down to the kitchen; I've never felt so naked in my

14

life. Of course I was naked – a sheet wrapped around me.
This glowering older brother had to go get my clothes,
unpinned the butterflies, who knows if they lived. I got the
whispering sister –
[LARRY. What a family!]
– to drop me off at the bus station; they were glad to get rid
of me. I was an hour and a half early, I didn't care. I drank
about twenty cups of that vending-machine coffee. Black;
the cream and sugar buttons didn't work. The bus-station
attendant is ogling me. I'm so wired from the caffeine, if
he'd said anything I'd have kneecapped him. There's these
two bag ladies yelling at each other, apparently they're
rivals. I fit right in.
[LARRY. Oh, God. To wake up to those – I can just see
them.]
Oh, Lord, I shrieked like a madwoman. They were glad to
get rid of me.

COMMENTARY: You need to consider Anna's state of mind as she
delivers this speech. It is late at night; the end of a hard day and a
terrifying week. She is tired, deeply upset and overwrought. The
story she tells, particularly the incident with the butterflies, is so
surreal it borders on hysteria. The whole tale unfolds like a bad
dream: mobs of people, the claustrophobia, the lies and hidden
secrets, the boy with the red hair, the butterflies, the lonely
episode in the bus station. Each event is full of very particular
details which give the different phases of the monologue richness
and specificity, saving it from becoming too sad and hysterical.
Anna has to compel us to listen to all the gothic details. The telling
of the story has to bring her to life.

Can't Stand Up for Falling Down
Richard Cameron

The Don Valley, South Yorkshire. A man's death has a profound effect on three young women.

Ruby (26) is a single mother with a seven-year-old son, Carl. She struggles to create a life for her son and dreams of being comfortably married. She has recently had an unsatisfactory relationship with a married man and is not optimistic about her prospects. She admits that her only true passion was for Royce, Carl's father, the violent town bully. When Royce discovered she was pregnant he offered to become engaged but only if she would declare that the child was not his. This she refused to do and so Royce walked out of her life. In this speech she reminisces about the early days of her pregnancy and her relationship with Royce when they were both eighteen.

RUBY. I knew for sure the day before Al Janney died. Aunt Madge said so. I wanted to ask her about it, but didn't. We sat in her little back room by the window, the table full of brasses that I dulled and she polished, and after a while of me thinking how I was going to tell her, she said,
'Does your mother know?'
and I said 'Does my mother know what?'
and she said 'Getting yourself pregnant'
and I said, 'Who says I am?'
and she said 'Aren't you?'

And I dulled a little brass ship and said 'Don't tell' and she said 'I won't if you don't want me to.'

I told her what I could and my fear went away and came on again in waves, but mostly I thanked God to have someone to talk to and whilst we talked I dulled and she polished. She asked me who it was and I couldn't tell her. Not before I told him. Tomorrow I'd tell him.

It was the Saturday that Al died. The day I went to tell Royce, when I was eighteen and expecting his baby and I had to ask him what I should do and I walked to their shop and just before I got there, I turned off, back along Church Lane and round, and on our road again, and past our house and up to the shop and turned off the other way and Saturday morning I walked miles to get to their shop up the road and when I got there it was closed for dinner.

Al was looking in the window. He had a little girl with him. I went down the alley to the back of the shop, up the yard and I could hear the radio playing in the back room.

John Farrow, Kite and Royce were playing cards and drinking beer. He laid a card and looked at me and the look said enough to make me want to go, and it was his turn to lay again and I turned away and he said 'Come here' and I came to him and stood by his chair and his hand went between my knees and stroked the front of my leg where they all could see.

'Don't', I said, and tried to pull away, but his hand held me fast and they smiled.

'Get us three pasties,' he said, and his hand that held me went into his back pocket and he put the money in my hand. I turned to go and he patted my behind.

I went to the butchers and got them. Al and the little girl were still at Royce's shop front. He was flapping the letter box. I went up to tell him to go but Royce opened the door and swore at him and pushed him away. I gave Royce the bag and said 'See you tonight,' and as he took the bag Al dodged into the shop. Royce went in and tried to chase him out, cursing.

And I walked home.

Ruby's life is severely limited. She exists in a world where a voice has a minimal function. It's difficult to speak, especially about personal tragedy, or to express feelings easily. Her monologue recalls a desperate attempt to tell first her aunt and then her lover that she is pregnant. Notice how abruptly and bluntly people in her world react. Conversations are over before they have barely begun. Neither Aunt Madge nor Royce make the time to give Ruby comfort. Aunt Madge is absorbed in polishing the brass and Royce in playing cards. Ruby is just an interruption in their routines.

———————

Lynette (22) has been Royce's wife for four years and they live above the fishing tackle shop that he runs. She has led a very circumscribed life, leaving school at fifteen to work at the local office of the Coal Board. When she married Royce he insisted that she cease working. Since then her lonely isolated life has been dominated by Royce. He is violent and vindictive towards her, finding fault with everything she does. She tries to remain optimistic that things will improve and seeks solace in prayer. As the violence increases she threatens to leave, but he intimidates her, saying that he will track her down wherever she goes. In this speech she reveals some of the stress she is under.

LYNETTE. Royce has now moved into the back bedroom, thank God. It's been a bit of a time, these last few weeks. I got a knife on the bedroom door lock and managed to get the paint off so it works, I can lock it at night now. Makes it a bit safer. I just don't know what he might do next, after the things he's said to me. Coming in, throwing things. Spoiling things in the house. What's the point of trying to keep things nice? I keep my room clean, I make my own meals when he's out. It's like a pigsty down there.

I tried to clean it up after he'd pulled everything out of the kitchen cupboard and smashed it, but I cut my hand quite bad on a bit of glass from the sauce bottle, I think it was, and I had to leave it. I should have had stitches really. It's funny, I thought it was tomato ketchup.

'Serves you fucking right,' he says. 'Cleaning up. You're always cleaning up. Leave it. Fucking LEAVE IT!' and something's exploded in my head and he must have hit my ear. My hand's full of blood but it's my ear that hurts. 'Don't you swear in this house! You stop saying your foul language to me, I won't have it. Don't swear!' and I'm hanging on to the edge of the sink to stop from falling over, I'm going dizzy. It makes me ill to hear bad words said before God and he knows it and he says it all the more, over and over, and my hand's under the tap and my head's swimming and ringing loud and the water turns red.

That night, I mend the door lock with one hand, while my other hand is throbbing through the cloth, and I hear him hammering and sawing in the shed in the yard, like it's been for days now into the night, but I don't care any more about what he's doing, I don't care, and I don't care if God doesn't want me to say it, I wish he were dead. I wish he were dead.

COMMENTARY: Lynette keeps herself isolated and behind defences until violence enters her life. Then the blur of arguments, physical abuse and a cut hand all work together to create a jumble of remembered pain. Though a woman of deep religious convictions, Lynette is also full of hatred and vengeance for a man who has made her life a misery. The remembered sound of him hammering and sawing in the shed, for what seemed like days, is a memory that continues to fuel her anger.

Cigarettes and Chocolate
Anthony Minghella

The garden of Gemma's north London flat.

Gemma (20s-30s) is a young urban professional who has a longterm relationship with Rob. To the amusement of their friends they do not actually live together but retain separate flats to avoid symbolic commitment. On returning from a holiday in Italy, Gemma completely stops speaking. She will neither speak to people directly nor answer the phone. This state of affairs has thrown all her friends and family into confusion. Each begins to feel that they are in some way guilty and responsible for her ominous silence. For Gemma this is a premeditated act. She marked in her calendar, with a big red cross, the day her silence would begin. It was to be 'like suicide in a way: to stop talking like killing oneself'. Prior to this she had been intensely passionate and committed to social and political ideals. She preferred a hands-on approach, favouring direct intervention and personal action instead of hollow gestures and glib liberal solutions. This dogged commitment and involvement would often irritate and annoy her friends. She is obsessed with Bach's 'St Matthew Passion' which she listens to over and over again, playing it whenever her friends stop by to try and talk her out of her silence. In this final speech of the play she confides in the audience.

GEMMA. When you stop speaking, it's like stopping eating. The first day there's something thrilling, and new, before the pain begins. The pain where you want to give up, where you can think of nothing else.

Then the second day, you feel wretched, the third delirious, and then suddenly there's no appetite, it shrinks, it shrinks, until the prospect of speaking, the thought of words retching from the mouth, how ugly and gross it seems.

Nothing changes.

How to stop people in their tracks, and make them think. Only if you're starving, if it's your son lying in your arms, or you think he might be in that discarded pile of mutilated bodies, or there's no milk in your breast and the baby's crying, or the radiation is leaking into your child's lungs, or the lead or the nitrates or the, or the, or the and all the while skirts get longer, skirts get shorter, skirts get longer, skirts get shorter, poetry is written, the news is read, I buy a different butter at the store and have my hair permed, straightened, coloured, cut, lengthened, all the while my hair keeps growing, I throw away all my skirts, a black bag to Oxfam, lately I've been at Oxfam buying back my skirts, I've stripped the pine and painted the pine, pulled out the fireplaces and put them back in, I'm on the pill, I'm off the pill, I'm on the pill, I'm off the pill. I'm listening to jazz, swing, jazz, swing, I'm getting my posters framed. I'm telling my women's group everything. I'm protesting. I'm protesting. I've covered my wall with postcards, with posters, with postcards, with posters. No this. Out them. In these. Yes those. No this. Out them. In these. Yes those. The rows. The rows with my friends, my lovers. What were they about? What did they change? The fact is, the facts are, nothing is changed. Nothing has been done. There is neither rhyme nor reason, just tears, tears, people's pain, people's rage, their aggression. And silence.

Look, already it's happening here, the weight of words, the torrent, all the words being said seep into each other, the rage, the protest all clotting together, sit and listen to the wireless and run the wheel of the tuner, spin the dial, hear them all at it, in all languages, pouring out. This is, after all, our first punishment – Babel – saying so much to say nothing. Doing so much to do nothing. Because the power to arrest, to stop us short in our tracks, what does that? (*Pause*.) but the silence, listen, how rich it is, how pregnant, how full . . . (*Pause*.)

What do you remember? When all is said an done? A

kiss? The taste of someone's lips? A view? A breath? A tune?
The weight of your grandmother's coffin? The veins on your
mother's legs. The white lines on her stomach.

Don't speak for a day and then start looking.

The senses are sharp. Look at the world about its
business. The snarl. The roar. Skin stretched over the teeth.
The madness.

The law is frightened of silence. It has words for the
defendant who becomes mute. The wrath of God. Mute by
malice. But it's not silence which is the punishment. Words.
WORDS are the punishment.
The silence.
(*A silence.*)
beautiful
last year it was cigarettes,
the year before chocolate
but this is the best
(*The Aria. 'Mache dich, Mein Hertze, Rein' from Bach's 'St
Matthew Passion'. Magnificent. Released.*)

COMMENTARY: Gemma takes us through the stages of going
silent. Part of her trauma is modern life and the inability of any
caring individual to effect change in the world. For Gemma words
have become a millstone. Talk has made her impotent ('saying so
much to say nothing . . . doing so much to do nothing'). At crucial
points in the speech the word 'nothing' surfaces, underlining the
nullity and void that lies at the heart of both the speech and
Gemma's predicament. Notice too that Gemma's sentences have a
tendency to trail off and lose power as silence gradually shrouds
her world. But just as the speech starts to empty out and lapse into
silence it begins to fill up again. Silence fills the void along with
other sense memories. Yet the fear and tyranny of words returns
and is suppresed again by silence. This is a difficult speech to get
right in performance. It's full of such stop-and-start, back-and-
forth repetitions. With all her macabre, dark images, Gemma
sounds like a penitent from another age.

The Conquest of the South Pole
Manfred Karge (translated by Tinch Minter and
Anthony Vivis)

Scene 3 (b): Hanging Out the Washing. Braukmann's attic.

*Luise Braukmann (20s) is married and works frying chips at an outdoor
stall. Her husband is unemployed and spends his days hanging out with
a gang of friends. She is a proud housewife and longs to have a child.
Despite her love for her husband he is beginning to get on her nerves.
While she is a pragmatic realist, Braukmann prefers to escape into a
world of fantasy and make-believe. She has just found her husband and
his pals horsing about in their attic and, after first chucking them out,
she lashes out at Braukmann in this speech.*

LA BRAUKMANN. I've had enough, Braukmann, I've
had enough. Pinball, schnaps, the end. Monkey business in
the attic. Who knows what's next? He's sunk to new depths,
that's what he's sunk to, new depths. You shudder to think,
that's what you shudder to do, think. It's enough to make
your blood run cold, your blood run cold is what it's enough
to make. When it comes to monkey business, Braukmann is
a star. He gives his all. As long as he's acting the fool. Then
he can dance. Then he can laugh. Then he's got something
to laugh about. But the rest of the time – There he sits,
gnawing his nails. There he glares, if you dare to talk to him.
There are his moods. Being unemployed just isn't fair, he
can't bear it. It's so bloody unfair he can't get his arse off the
chair any more, can't speak for despair. There he is
suffering. There he is, being Gandhi. But any chance of
monkey business and he's raring to go. Never a care. There
he's got flair. I've had enough, Braukmann, I've had
enough. (BRAUKMANN *goes out.*) When we were kids we

23

always used to play Stay-where-you-are-and-don't-move-a-muscle. When Mother came up the creaky old stairs, we made ourselves scarce. The attic was out of bounds. Up here was the only place the coal dust couldn't blow about as it did below. And Mother was constantly washing. Constantly washing and wiping. Always up and at it. Father's things in particular she was constantly washing. She'd stuck a post-card behind the mirror. There was a mountain on it, covered with ice and snow. White, everything white, she once said, chance would be a fine thing. The washing and wiping I inherited. Grease is what I'm up against. Given the choice between hairdressing and chip-frying, I said to myself, I'd rather touch greasy chips than greasy chaps. Now I'm up to my eye-balls in grease. But I picked up a trick from a film. Get back from work, strip off, rub myself all over with a hefty chunk of lemon. The bird in the film sold fish not chips, but fish or fat it still does the trick. I'm for films. But I can't ever get Braukmann to go to the cinema. The one time I did, the film was about a bloke who was unemployed, and before you could blink, he was off. He won't face it, he can't face it. Sometimes he just sits at the table cowering, and stares at the wall. Just sits there cowering and stares at the wall. Bad, really bad. I can't help him. And he just sits there cowering and stares at the wall.

COMMENTARY: Luise's speech sizzles and spatters like the chips she fries. She's lost patience with a useless husband and a life that seems to be leading to a dead end. The final line of the speech tells where the words are heading: to a blank wall. But in the midst of Luise's anger the image of a white, snow-covered mountain looms. It shifts the terms of speech from drudgery to momentary awe and escape. But then it is back to hackneyed routine, signalled by her use of short, sharp declarative sentences in which the same words are recycled over and over. The structure of the sentences also give the speech its peculiar staccato rhythm.

Death and the Maiden
Ariel Dorfman

Act 1, scene 4. The time is the present and the place, a country that is probably Chile, but could be any country that has given itself a democratic government just after a long period of dictatorship. The terrace of the Escobars' beach house. Before dawn.

Paulina Escobar (around 40 years old) is married to Gerardo who, under the dictatorship, was an enemy of the state. Paulina's career as a student doctor was abruptly cut short when she was arrested by the police, tortured and raped. Gerardo is a lawyer who has just been appointed to head a commission investigating the crimes of the recent dictatorship. When Gerardo's car breaks down Roberto Miranda, a doctor, gives him a lift. On arriving home Gerardo then invites Roberto to stay the night. Paulina does not directly meet Roberto, but she is seen listening to the two men as they chat on the terrace. As she listens she becomes convinced from the familiarity of his voice that Roberto was her chief torturer and she decides to take vengeance on him. Early the following morning she goes into Roberto's room, drags him out to the terrace, ties him to a chair with a pair of stockings and gags him with her panties. The speech that follows is her first verbal attack on him.

ROBERTO *opens his eyes. He tries to get up and realises that he is tied. He begins to roll over and desperately try to free himself.* PAULINA *is sitting in front of him with her gun.* ROBERTO *looks at her with a terrorised expression in his eyes.*
PAULINA (*very calm*). Good morning, Dr . . . Miranda, isn't it? Dr Miranda. (*She shows him the gun and points it playfully in his direction.*) I had a chum from the University, name of Miranda, Maria Elena Miranda, you wouldn't be

25

related to the Mirandas of San Esteban, would you? She had quite a mind. A marvellous retentive memory, we used to call her our little encyclopaedia. I have no idea what became of her. She probably finished her medical studies, became a doctor, just like you.

I didn't get my diploma . . . I didn't get too far with my studies, Dr Miranda. Let's see if you can guess why I didn't get my diploma, I'm pretty sure that it won't take a colossal effort of the imagination on your part to guess why.

Luckily there was Gerardo. He was – well, I wouldn't exactly say he was waiting for me – but let's say that he still loved me, so I never had to go back to the Universtity. Lucky for me, because I felt – well, phobia wouldn't be the right word, a certain apprehension – about medicine. I wasn't so sure about my chosen profession. But life is never over till it's over, as they say. That's why I'm wondering whether it might not be a good idea to sign up again – you know, ask that I be readmitted. I read the other day, now that the military aren't in charge anymore, that the University has begun to allow the students who were kicked out to apply for readmittance.

But here I am chatting away when I'm supposed to make breakfast, aren't I, a nice breakfast? Now you like – let's see, ham with mayonnaise, wasn't that it? Ham with mayonnaise sandwiches. We haven't got mayonnaise, but we do have ham. Gerardo also likes ham. I'll get to know your other tastes. Sorry about the mayonnaise. I hope you don't mind that this must remain, for the moment, a monologue. You'll have your say, Doctor, you can be sure of that. I just don't want to remove this – gag, you call it, don't you? – at least not till Gerardo wakes up. But I should be getting him up. Did I tell you I phoned the garage from the call box? They'll be here soon. (*She goes to the bedroom door, unlocks it, opens it.*) The real real truth is that you look slightly bored. (*Takes a cassette out of her pocket.*) I took this

26

out of your car – I took the liberty – what if we listen to some Schubert while I make breakfast, a nice breakfast, Doctor? 'Death and the Maiden'? (*She puts it into the cassette-player. We begin to hear Schubert's quartet 'Death and the Maiden'.*) D'you know how long it's been since I last listened to this quartet? If it's on the radio, I switch it off, I even try not to go out much, though Gerardo has all these social events he's got to attend and if they ever name him Minister we're going to live running around shaking hands and smiling at perfect strangers, but I always pray they won't put on Schubert. One night we were dining with – they were extremely important people, and our hostess happened to put Schubert on, a piano sonata, and I thought, do I switch it off or do I leave, but my body decided for me, I felt extremely ill right then and there and Gerardo had to take me home, so we left them there listening to Schubert and nobody knew what had made me ill, so I pray they won't play that anywhere I go, any Schubert at all, strange isn't it, when he used to be, and I would say, yes I really would say, he's still my favourite composer, such a sad, noble sense of life. But I always promised myself a time would come to recover him, bring him back from the grave so to speak, and just sitting here listening to him with you I know that I was right, that I'm – so many things that are going to change from now on, right? To think I was on the verge of throwing my whole Schubert collection out, crazy! (*Raising her voice, to* GERARDO.) Isn't this quartet marvellous, my love. (*To* ROBERTO.) And now I'll be able to listen to my Schubert again, even go to a concert like we used to. Did you know that Schubert was homosexual? But of course you do, you're the one who kept repeating it over and over in my ear over and over again while you played 'Death and the Maiden'. Is this the very cassette, Doctor, or do you buy a new one every year to keep the sound pure?

COMMENTARY: All of Paulina's hopes, beliefs and aspirations were destroyed by the sadistic torture she received. Whenever she talks every word and phrase appears to be loaded with menacing vengeance. Life no longer has normal values because her brush with death was too profound. In this speech the convention seems to be one of polite conversation; a hostess talking to her guest. But you are also stalking your victim and enjoying your new-found position of power. You are making him feel both at ease but also off-balance. She plays a cat and mouse game. The music Paulina plays is the same piece of Schubert her torturer played while he administered pain. So the quartet when heard has a shocking and debilitating effect on Paulina. It is also the proof she needs to say that Roberto is guilty. By the end of the speech Paulina is right by Roberto's ear, duplicating the relationship she once had as victim to her torturer. The actor should realize that Paulina has been up all night plotting her revenge.

Decadence
Steven Berkoff

Scene 1. Black floor, white set with a white leather sofa.

Helen (30s) is a sophisticated upper-class woman. She is devoted to living a carefree luxurious lifestyle. She thinks only of her own comfort and immediate sensory gratification. Her conversation is peppered with references to all the 'in' designers, restaurants and resorts. Hers is a life of aimless leisure and sybaritic pleasure. She is having an affair with Steve, a married man. This speech opens the play. Steve is on the sofa and remains frozen until after she finishes speaking. She wears a sexy black dress.

HELEN. How sweet of you to come on time/bastard! sweet darling! my you do look so divine. I've been so bored/have a drink/what . . . ?/Of course! a Drambuie with soda and a splash of Cinzano . . . with masses of ice/I've been so bored tearing round to find just what would enchant you to eat me for breakfast (*Raising skirt.*) *charmant n'est-ce pas*/does it make you go all gooey/does it send spasms up and down your spine/enough ice! sweety you do look nice. Do you like my legs?/aren't my frillies sweet/does it make you get just a little on heat/kiss me/gently/don't smudge now/just a touch/a graze won't be a trice/I'll get ready/so late I couldn't find a fucking taxi/oh I hate to miss the first scene the first embrace/what's that we're seeing/the name of the play!/taxis were thin on the ground/outside Harrods there were none around/I stretched out an arm/I felt like Moses/what did he do/raise his arms to heaven for the Hebrews/the longer he kept his arm in the air the better would his armies fare, but when it fell wearily down/bloody nosed moishers and crunch smash and pound/you've not said a word/but you do look dishy/a bird in the ice floes/or chilled meringue frappé/you look simply gay/got a fag . . . hmm! Smoke gets in your eyes! Shit! Oh sorry/tit! Ready heart? Where for dinner after/surprise me then, give me a thrill/so long as I gorge on some juicy meat/I'm as hungry as a vampire/if I don't eat soon I'll simply expire/did you have a nice day/little wife all safe and tucked away/come open your mouth and dazzle my ears/come love . . . /you look troubled/close to tears/what have I done . . . shit . . . you look bad/what's the matter hone(y)?

COMMENTARY: The playwright says that the 'Acting should be sensual, erotic, flamboyant.' The speech is full of direct address and asides. The acting is double-edged. The verse structure of the speech gives it an oddly epic quality, best seen in allusions to Moses parting the Red Sea. The speech is also full of movement as Helen flits around; the perfect mistress, attending to Steve's every whim and wish. She's also rapacious about food, drink and shopping. Yet there is also something vulgar and low about Helen when she resorts to profanity. Suddenly the sexy, sophisticated illusion is shattered. In performing this speech you must maintain the illusion of being a solicitous mistress and also undercut it with Helen's selfish vanity. The speech, like the whole play, has an animal-like quality as the two characters prey on and paw one another.

Digging for Fire
Declan Hughes

Act 1, scene 2. The dining room in a house a couple of miles south of Dublin. An evening in July.

Emily (early 30s) is an artist. She has been living in New York for the past couple of years, but she has returned to Dublin for a brief visit. Her friends Brendan and Clare are hosting a reunion for their mates from university days. Although their lives have all gone in quite different routes, Brendan likes to bring them all together for old time's sake to compare notes and score points off one another. They have all been drinking 'exotic beers'. In this speech Emily describes how she found success in New York.

EMILY: Well . . . ah it's all so corny, it's like Lana Turner on the stool at Schwab's. I'm serving in the cafe one day, and of course the whole place is like some home for the deluded anyway – no-one *really* works there – here's a writer, there's an actress, hello you pair of poets – standard young hopeful stuff. So I'm serving, and this dapper little faggot is really hassling me . . .
[BREDA. (I hate that word, faggot.)
RORY. (I'm rather fond of it, actually.)]
Now I know this guy a little, I don't know who he is, but he knows I paint, and we'd made small talk about the scene before, bitchy stuff mostly. But suddenly he's being really obnoxious, like 'This glass is *not* clean', and 'I don't *believe* this oregano is fresh', and 'I really *need* a raspberry vinaigrette', and so on, and the cafe is *bunged* so we're all having a ball. Comes to the coffee, he wants a double expresso, decaff., which to me is like having sex with all your clothes on. Anyway, our owner being something of a coffee zealot,

there isn't any decaff. on the premises, so he gets an ordinary expresso. Seconds later, these *squeals* suddenly go up, he's shrieking like a stuck pig, 'This is not decaff., this is caffeinated, I wanted decaff.', and I have had it, I stand there 'till he's quietened down, and then I say 'Listen, you big fat baby, why don't you just suck my dick?' (*Pause*.)
[RORY. Well what else *could* you have said, dear?]
Turns out this guy – Roland Michaels – owns the West 4th Street Gallery. Turns out also he's the kind of queen who keeps Bette Midler in diamonds, he loves a girl with a dirty mouth. I'm cleaning his table, he's left a $20 tip and his card, and written on the back of the card is 'If you paint as tough as you talk, I'm interested. Call me tomorrow.' I called, he saw, he offered. And four months later, I had my first show.

COMMENTARY: Emily has all the hard-won off-handedness of someone who's been through hard times. (We later learn that she is HIV-positive and she says in typical fashion: 'It's not a metaphor. It's just bad luck.') How true or manufactured the details of this story are is up to the performer to decide. Basically this is the tale of 'how I was discovered'. So you really want to milk all the details, realizing that you are speaking to a room full of savvy, witty friends all of whom lust after fame and success. They hang on Emily's every camp word. There are two parts to be played here – Emily and the man – and the whole scene is carefully laid-out in the opening moments. The payoff lines are very simple, clipped and triumphant.

Etta Jenks
Marlane Meyer

Scene 2. A room in a house in Los Angeles.

*Etta Jenks (early 30s) has come to Los Angeles with the dream of
becoming a movie star. She has never actually trained or worked as an
actress. She has had a series of jobs including two-and-a-half years as an
usherette and a couple of months working behind a luncheonette counter.
She has an unconventional family background: her parents were brother
and sister and she was born out of wedlock and in incest. Etta also had a
child but she put it up for adoption at birth. She lives in the present and
thinks only of the future; for Etta her unusual background is merely
historical fact which has no place in her new life. She is without
emotions. When she arrives by train in Los Angeles she has no place to
stay and only a couple of hundred dollars in her pocket. She asks a
luggage handler, Burt, who is deaf, to help her find somewhere to stay.
He takes her to the house of his blind twin brother Sherman who rents out
rooms. After several weeks her money is beginning to run out and she is
finding it much harder than she expected to get work. 'She spends hours
making up. Even when there's no place to go. She likes to look her best.'
She hates sex but knows that she is good at it. She seduces Burt on her
first night in Los Angeles. In this scene Etta is wearing a slip and as she
sets her hair with hot rollers she talks to Burt.*

ETTA. I think my throat is closing up. Those french fries
were so dry, I think they're caught . . . like a lump in my
throat. (*She nudges* BURT.) I think those fries got caught in
my throat.
[BURT. Drink water.]
I wish I had a Coke. I saw this science experiment once,
where they put this tooth in Coke, and over a period of a few
weeks or days . . . or maybe it was just one day, it
completely fell apart. Just disappeared.

33

I guess that could happen with a whole set of teeth if we were to sit around with a mouth full of Coca-Cola day and night. I wonder how it would work, the teeth comin' out, would you swallow and then what, would they come back in . . . somehow?

God, I'm stupid. What am I supposed to do? I thought by now I'd at least have some kinda extra work, somethin' . . .

I met this girl, Sheri, at the lunch counter? I thought she was pretty weird but she came out to be nice and she said that one way to break into movies is to have a videotape of yourself made.

Performing a scene with someone or maybe doin' a monologue. But the problem is, it cost. I wonder how I could get five hundred dollars?

I had four hundred, but that's just about gone. I wonder if I could find somebody with one of those video cameras you use at home? (*She nudges* BURT, *he looks at her.*) Do you know anybody with a . . . home-movie camera?

COMMENTARY: Throughout the play Etta speaks in an impersonal manner. She's single-minded and constantly focused only on herself: what is happening to her body and how she can break into films. Other people don't really matter very much except as a means to this end. She also speaks in grotesque and foul images (the 'french fries' and the 'tooth in Coke') and this queasy side of life seems to fascinate her. Part of Etta is still a selfish teenager. Notice how she jumps from point to point without any rhyme or reason. At first she's just killing time aimlessly chatting but her tone shifts and she becomes much more decisive when she focuses on her own career. That's it, she decides, I'll get a camera and make my own tape.

The Fastest Clock in the Universe
Philip Ridley

Act 2. A dilapidated room above an abandoned abattoir in the East End of London.

Sherbet Gravel 'is seventeen years old, long curly red hair, with lots of glamorous make-up. She is wearing a white uniform, stilettos and clutching a large, black handbag'. She works in a beauty salon. She is pregnant and engaged to the sixteen-year-old Foxtrot Darling. Foxtrot has been lured to a nineteenth birthday party by Cougar Glass who intends to seduce him. The thirty-year-old Cougar lives in a bizarre relationship with Captain Tock and dreams of outwitting age, remaining eternally a teenager. Foxtrot innocently brings Sherbet along to the party. Her arrival sends Cougar into a jealous sulk. The Captain exults as he sees Cougar's frustration. Under Sherbet's direction the celebrations continue despite Cougar's petulant, silent withdrawal. After the guests blow out the candles on Cougar's birthday cake, Sherbet first persuades the Captain to reveal what his one wish would be and then she too reveals her wish.

SHERBET. Who wants to know my wish?
[CAPTAIN. Me, please.
SHERBET. Babe?
FOXTROT. What?]
Do you want to know my wish?
[FOXTROT. All right.
SHERBET. All right what?
FOXTROT. All right Babe.]
I wish to grow old gracefully. Now I know that sounds ridiculous, but I've seen enough people not doing it gracefully to know what I'm talking about. The beauty salon where I work is full of them. Men and women, all with the

35

same look in their eyes. Make me young, says the look. But you know something? There's nothing we can do. Nature has rules and regulations and most of them are either cruel or very cruel. You know, I can usually tell a person's age as easy as that! One look is all it takes. There's this one woman who comes in – I feel sorry for her in a way – and she's got this photograph of what she looked like when she was nineteen. She must be fifty if she's a day now. Anyway, she comes in and she shows me this photograph and – fucking hell! – was she beautiful! 'This was me', she says. It's as if that photograph captured her at the happiest moment of her life. Perhaps it's like that. Perhaps we reach our peak when we're nineteen and, for one glorious summer, we're in control of our lives, and we look wonderful and everything is perfect. And then it's never the same again. And we spend the rest of our lives merely surviving one empty summer after another.

COMMENTARY: Though still young, Sherbet speaks with world-weary wisdom. She's bossy, brassy and talkative. Tart of tongue and of looks, she uses her East End accent and cheekiness to bizarre effect. But there is something deadly sour about the seemingly sweet Sherbet. In fact, she's really very deadly. Her speech grows in its sense of desolation. Each of her sentences probably evokes a reaction in Cougar. She wants her words to have an effect. She also knows what people are really looking for: eternal youth, their lost youth, a perfect moment at nineteen. In her hands this knowledge is a powerful weapon which she uses against the ageing and increasingly desperate Cougar. In the world of this play time and nature take their toll.

Frankie and Johnny in the Clair de Lune
Terrence McNally

Act 2. Frankie's one-room apartment in a walk-up tenement in New York City. The present. Very early Sunday morning.

Frankie (37) has 'striking but not conventional good looks. She has a sense of humour and a fairly tough exterior. She is also frightened and can be very hard to reach.' She works as a waitress in a luncheonette. She has come home with Johnny, the new short-order cook. They make love and spend a considerable time talking and getting to know one another. It starts as a one night stand but develops into something more meaningful, as the talkative, self-taught Johnny tries to 'connect' with Frankie. She is cautious and tries to resist his heartfelt romantic approach. At one point Johnny phones up a radio station to make a request for a record and sums up their relationship to the DJ. 'There's a man and a woman. Not young, not old. No great beauties, either one. They meet where they work: a restaurant and it's not the Ritz. She's a waitress. He's a cook. They meet but they don't connect. "I got two medium burgers working" and "Pick up, side of fries" is pretty much the extent of it. But she's noticed him, he can feel it. And he's noticed her. Right off. They both knew tonight was going to happen. So why did it take him six weeks for him to ask her if she wanted to see a movie that neither one of them could tell you the name of right now? . . . And then they were making love and for maybe an hour they forgot the ten million things that made them think "I don't love this person. I don't even like them" and instead all they knew was that they were perfect and that's all there was to know about it and as they lay there, they both began the million reasons not to love one another like a familiar rosary.' Their second attempt at love-making stalls when Johnny fails to get an erection. As Frankie teases him he gets defensive, arguing that this is the first time it has ever happened to him. In this speech she tries to explain a possible cause of his impotence.

[JOHNNY. You're lucky women don't have problems like this.

FRANKIE. We've got enough of our own in that department.

JOHNNY. It's male menopause. I've been dreading this.]

FRANKIE. You know what I think it was? The moonlight. You were standing in it. It was bathing your body. I've always been very suspicious of what moonlight does to people.

[JOHNNY. It's supposed to make them romantic.]

Or turn you into a werewolf. That's what I was raised on. My grandmother was always coming into my bedroom to make sure the blinds were down. She was convinced sleeping in the moonlight would turn you into the wolfman. I thought if I slept in the moonlight I'd wake up a beautiful fairy princess, so I kept falling asleep with the blinds open and she kept coming in and closing them. She always denied it was her. 'Wasn't me, precious. Must have been your Guardian Angel.' Remember them?

[JOHNNY. What do you mean, 'remember'?]

One night I decided to stay awake and catch her in the act. It seemed like forever. When you're that age, you don't have anything to stay awake *about*. So you're failing geography, so what? Finally my grandmother came into the room. She had to lean across my bed to close the blinds. Her bosom was so close to my face. She smelled so nice. I pretended I was still sleeping and took the deepest breath of her I could. In that one moment, I think I knew what it was like to be loved. Really loved. I was so safe, so protected! That's better than being pretty. I'll never forget it. The next thing I knew it was morning and I still didn't look like Audrey Hepburn. Now when I lie in bed with the blinds up and the moonlight spilling in, I'm not thinking I want to be somebody else, I just want my Nana back.

COMMENTARY: Frankie describes a comforting, tender scene from childhood. At this point in her relationship with Johnny, all the various memories of love come welling forth. The story about the moonlight and childhood is meant to comfort Johnny but ultimately becomes a tale about Frankie's own vulnerable feelings about her looks and the loss of her grandmother. It almost sounds like an episode from a fairy tale. She isolates a moment when she felt totally loved and protected, and she tries to hold the moment for as long as she can. Throughout the play Frankie has been denying love. Now she reaches out to embrace it.

Giving Notes
Victoria Wood

A rehearsal hall. This is a stand-up routine performed entirely on its own.

Alma, a middle-aged sprightly woman, addresses her amateur company after a rehearsal of Hamlet. She claps her hands.

ALMA. Right. Bit of hush please. Connie! Thank you. Now that was quite a good rehearsal; I was quite pleased. There were a few raised eyebrows when we let it slip the Piecrust Players were having a bash at Shakespeare but I think we're getting there. But I can't say this too often: it may be *Hamlet* but it's got to be Fun Fun Fun! (*She consults her notes.*) Now we're still very loose on lines. Where's Gertrude? I'm not so worried about you – if you 'dry' just give us a bit of business with the shower cap. But Barbara – you will have to buckle down. I mean, Ophelia's mad scene, 'There's rosemary, that's for remembrance' – it's no good just bunging a few herbs about and saying, 'Don't mind me, I'm a loony'. Yes? You see, this is our marvellous bard, Barbara, you cannot paraphrase. It's not like Pinter where you can more or less say what you like as long as you leave enough gaps.

Right, Act One, Scene One, on the ramparts. Now I know the whist table is a bit wobbly, but until Stan works out how to adapt the Beanstalk it'll have to do. What's this? Atmosphere? Yes – now what did we work on, Philip? Yes, it's midnight, it's jolly cold. What do we do when it's cold? We go 'Brrr', and we do this. (*Slaps hands on arms.*) Right, well don't forget again, please. And cut the hot-water bottle, it's not working.

Where's my ghost of Hamlet's father? Oh yes, what went wrong tonight, Betty? He's on nights still, is he? OK. Well, it's not really on for you to play that particular part, Betty – you're already doing the Player Queen and the back legs of Hamlet's donkey. Well, we don't know he didn't have one, do we? Why waste a good cossy?

Hamlet – drop the Geordie, David, it's not coming over. Your characterization's reasonably good, David, but it's just far too gloomy. Fair enough, make him a little bit depressed at the beginning, but start lightening it from Scene Two, from the hokey-cokey onwards, I'd say. And perhaps the, er, 'Get thee to a nunnery' with Ophelia – perhaps give a little wink to the audience, or something, because he's really just having her on, isn't he, we decided . . .

Polonius, try and show the age of the man in your voice and in your bearing, rather than waving the bus-pass. I think you'll find it easier when we get the walking frame. Is that coming, Connie? OK.

The Players' scene: did any of you feel it had stretched a bit too . . . ? Yes. I think we'll go back to the tumbling on the entrance, rather than the extract from *Barnum*. You see, we're running at six hours twenty now, and if we're going to put those soliloquies back in . . .

Gravediggers? Oh yes, gravediggers. The problem here is that Shakespeare hasn't given us a lot to play with – I feel we're a little short on laughs, so Harold, you do your dribbling, and Arthur, just put in anything you can remember from the Ayckbourn, yes?

The mad scene: apart from lines, much better, Barbara – I can tell you're getting more used to the straitjacket. Oh – any news on the skull, Connie? I'm just thinking, if your little dog pulls through, we'll have to fall back on papier mâché. All right, Connie, as long as it's dead by the dress . . .

Oh yes, Hamlet, Act Three, Scene One, I think that cut works very well, 'To be or not to be', then Ophelia comes straight in, it moves it on, it's more pacey . . .

Act Five, Gertrude, late again. What? Well, is there no service wash? I'm sure Dame Edith wasn't forever nipping out to feed the dryer.

That's about it – oh yes, Rosencrantz and Guildenstern, you're not on long, make your mark. I don't think it's too gimmicky, the tandem. And a most important general note – make-up! Half of you looked as if you hadn't got any on! And Claudius – no moles again? (*Sighs*.) I bet Margaret Lockwood never left hers in the glove compartment.

That's it for tonight then; thank you. I shall expect you to be word-perfect by the next rehearsal. Have any of you realised what date we're up to? Yes, April the twenty-seventh! And when do we open? August! It's not long!

COMMENTARY: The comedy here is in the situation and words and doesn't need to be overplayed by the actor. It's very easy to let the outrageousness of the situation run away with itself. The character of Alma, a lively provincial committee woman with a touch of the schoolmistress, should be drawn from life; we've all met an Alma. She's a complete amateur who has no business directing Shakespeare. In fact, her approach to *Hamlet* is to stress the 'ham'! One aspect of the speech that must be obeyed in order to keep it in bounds is that Alma and her inexperienced cast are all on the same confused level, sitting in the same leaking boat that is in the process of sinking. She can't quite figure out what is wrong with the production or how to help the actors with their dreadful performances. She just tells them to do more of this or less of that. The effort everyone is putting out is in indirect proportion to the task before them: to produce a great classic. Throughout Alma is referring to her notes, so each paragraph of the speech is directed at a different cast member.

Her Aching Heart
Bryony Lavery

Chapter One: A Nun Has A Nightmare

Molly (18) is a votive nun. She is a character in a Barbara Cartlandish lesbian romantic novel. She is 'dressed in a shift. Her heart is aching. Anguish clouds her sweet eyes'. She is a simple, good-hearted, innocent village girl. In this speech she reveals some of her repressed passions.

MOLLY. Last night I dreamt I went to Helstone Hall again. It seemed to me I stood before the intricately-wrought iron gate leading to the densely-wooded drive, and for a while I could not enter for the way was barred to me. There was a lock and chain keeping shut the gate. I called in my dream to the lodge-keeper . . . crusty, kindly Samuel, 'Helloooo! Let me by!' But no answer came and peering through the rusted rococo I saw that Samuel's cheery cottage was empty. No smoke curled from the chimney. No smell of baking bread issued from the gaping door. No comfort met me.

Then, like all dreamers, I was possessed of a sudden with supernatural powers . . . and I passed like a spirit through the gate and was racing, like a thing possessed, up the twisting drive. Past the gnarled oaks choked with ivy. Past the rhododendron bushes twisted and tortured. Past the bracken rank and wild. And I stood before the mighty, looming presence of Helstone Hall. (*She clutches at her heart.*) Ooooooooh! Dear Watcher, it was EMPTY!!!!! The Great Lawn, once smooth and green as a billiard table . . . was tossed and torn with mole-mounds . . . The soaring grey-granite walls were choked and poked with thrusting tendrils of ivy . . . The mullioned windows, once twinkling

43

with bubbled bright glass, were broken, dark . . . like blinded eyes. Helstone Hall was an empty shell, just as is now my breast where once beat my gentle heart. (*Her tears flow, like the River Dart, fast and furious. She picks up a black garment, wipes her eyes upon it. She puts it on.*) Moonlight can play odd tricks upon the fancy . . . for in my dream, excitement rippled through my slight form . . . and I could swear the house was not empty . . . but pulsed with life . . . Pungent woodsmoke puffed from the myriad chimney pots, warm light from many-branched silver candlesticks streamed from the windows and the warm night air carried the sound of human voices. (*There is the sound of human voices.*) The wild and extravagant Helstones down from London with their rakish friends . . . the rich and dissolute men, (*She puts on a white close-fitting hood.*) the beautiful powdered women (*She puts on a cross.*) and at the centre of that glittering throng rich and lovely ardent and wilful the impetuous Lady Harriet Helstone. (*She puts on a wimple.*) Harriet. (*With warm affection.*) Harriet. (*With lust.*) Harriet. (*With longing.*) Harriet. (*With hatred.*) Harriet. (*With emptiness.*) Harriet. (*She picks up a Bible and exits.*)

COMMENTARY: What's so wonderful about this speech – apart from its parody of romantic gothic fiction – is that it tells a complete story. It takes the listener on an entrancing journey in which events are seen and experienced. It calls for brisk, transformational acting. At times the pace creeps for the sake of tension and then speeds along. Different emotions are catalogued in the performance. In acting this speech you are not aiming for humour and parody, but trying to contain the adventurous spirit of a heroine who is set free to make her way in a world of fantasy and love. To help you in this journey, the writer has filled the speech with appropriate sound effects, scene and costume changes.

Here
Michael Frayn

Act 2, scene 1. An empty room.

Pat (50s) is a widowed landlady. This room, which she rents to a young couple, and the rest of her house are like a scrapbook of family memories. Each room has an anecdotal association for her. Although she lives in the past she has no regrets and certainly does not envy the young couple, Cath and Phil, as they make their start in life. At regular intervals she pops in for a chat or to offer the loan of a piece of furniture – much to the irritation of the couple. In this scene she is chatting wih Cath about the territorial nature of relationships.

PAT. . . . You divide things up.
[CATH. This is him, here, up to an imaginary line on this side of the bed.]
I was the windows. Anything to do with the windows – that was me. He always blamed me for the windows. So that was *my* fault, of course, when the sash broke, and the window came down on top of him.
[CATH. *He's* the windows. I'm the curtains.]
No, I was always the windows. Windows and door-handles. And the roof. And the fireplaces. Because he liked modern, you see, Eric. He was always for modern. So anything that wasn't modern in the house, and it went wrong, that was my fault. He'd sit there reading his paper and I'd know something was up just from the look on his face. So I wouldn't say anything – I wouldn't give him the satisfaction. I'd wait. He'd go on reading the paper, not a word, just this tight little look, and I'd know he'd got this wonderful grievance. I'd wait. *He'd* wait. Then just as I was going out of the room, say, just as I was putting the supper on the

45

table, out it would bounce. 'The bedroom door-handle,' he'd say. It used to make me so cross! 'The bedroom door-handle.' Like that. As soon as he said it I could feel my muscles all clench up. I'd just stop where I was, look at him, wait, not say anything. 'It's loose, it's going to come off,' he'd say. And so pleased with himself! Always knew I'd got a bad character, and now here I was, caught in the act, letting the bedroom door-handle get loose. So of course I wouldn't admit it. Nothing to do with me! 'Oh,' I'd say, 'is it really? Then why don't you get upstairs and mend it?' But inside, Cath, inside, I knew he was right, I knew it was me that had done it, because if it was the door-handle then it had to be me. So he wouldn't mend it, and I wouldn't get Mr Weeks to do it, and he'd sigh and raise his eyebrows every time he put his hand on it, and not say anything, and I'd look the other way, and not say anything, until in the end it'd fall off, and then at last, with a special holy look like Jesus picking up the cross, he'd get the toolbox out, and there wouldn't be any screws in the tin, so he'd have to do it with three nails and some glue instead, and there'd be blood dripping on the carpet, only he wouldn't let me put a plaster on it for him, and then I *couldn't* tell Mr Weeks about it when he came to do the boiler because that'd look as if I was criticising his handiwork and turning up my nose at the great sacrifice he'd made even though he was in the right and I was in the wrong. (*Pause.*) The boiler, that was me as well.

[CATH. I'm the soap, I don't know why.]

The boiler, the drain outside the back door. Yes, I don't know why I was the drain.

[CATH. The soap and the towels.]

But then *he* was the lights and the washing-machine. Oh yes. All the machines, all the electrical. Anything modern, you see. He'd come home in the evening – darkness. 'That washing machine,' I'd say before he could so much as open his mouth. 'You'll have to do something about it, Eric. Water all over the floor. Flash! Crack! I wonder it didn't kill me.' And at once he'd go mad. 'There's nothing wrong with the machine,' he'd say. 'It's what you ask it to do.' Shouting away at me. Because he knew it was his fault, you see, the washing-machine. If it was a gadget, if it was labour-saving, then that was his responsibility. Poor Eric. Poor old boy. But you can't take the blame for everything, can you, Cath. You've got to divide things up.

COMMENTARY: Pat encapsulates a life lived as a thing ('I was the windows . . . roof and fireplaces'). Her speech is rattled off as if it is a well-remembered routine. Nothing in what she says points to a tender human moment but just to a series of episodes in which things break down and nothing gets mended. We connect with what she says because we are all victims of similar household failures that put pressure on relationships. Beneath all her chatter, though, you know that Pat is describing an alienated relationship in which both spouses have severely compartmentalized each other's roles and functions. They are a divided couple. Each banality is given tragic weight.

Hush
April de Angelis

Act 1, scene 9. A room in a house which looks dusty and unlived in.

Denise (20s-30s), when asked, says she 'does house craft' but to everyone around her she is a treasured cleaner. She wants to fulfill herself in some other way and dreams of going to Tibet to find her real self. She is very attracted to New Age thinking. She is friendly and chatty but in a self-absorbed way. She has met a man on the beach and she hopes, though she never actually invited him, that he will unexpectedly drop round to see her. In anticipation she has put on a short dress and made herself up. In this speech she offers an explanation for 'the bit' of a depression which had once caused her to get 'really pissed'.

DENISE. The reason I'd been depressed was because I'd been working at this sandwich-making job. I was living with this bloke and we were making sandwiches in his flat. At first I really threw myself into it. I experimented with fillings, I bought a butter dish. We used to drive round delivering sandwiches to local businesses only quite often we never got any orders. We ate quite a lot of sandwiches on those occasions. That dealt quite a blow to my enthusiasm, I can tell you. Not to mention the fact that I wasn't getting the correct balance of amino acids in my diet. And that can lead to personality disorders. Like shoplifting or slimming. Then one day we found a cockroach lying upside down in a giant size tub of margarine. It wasn't me that left the lid off. That was when the infestation started. You can never be alone with an infestation. Soon after that he left me. He walked out leaving rent arrears and twenty-seven kilos of cheddar. I lay in bed weeping for days. I don't know if what we had was love but it did provide light relief from all the buttering. That was before I became a Buddhist. I used to watch the cockroaches basking on the walls. They do say in the event of a nuclear holocaust cockroaches will survive to inherit the earth. They used to crawl around in a superior manner as if they knew they could survive intense heat and I couldn't. Cocky bastards. The thing is, I'd never go through that now. Be used like that. Because now I'm different. Transformed by experience.

COMMENTARY: Denise tries to make light of a chain of events in her life: the failure of a relationship. The sheer drudgery and routine of the sandwich-making job, the cockroach infestation, the lying in bed for days weeping must all be lived through again when delivering this speech. The speech also reveals how angry she is that the relationship did not work out. She dwells, for instance, on the cockroaches – almost blaming them for her man's desertion. She delivers the speech while she waits, in keen anticipation, for a new man to pay her a visit. So her anxiety is very heightened.

The Last Yankee
Arthur Miller

Act 1, scene 2. Patricia Hamilton's bedroom in a state mental hospital in New England.

Patricia Hamilton (44) is clinically depressed and has been a patient at the hospital for the past seven weeks. She has been married for twenty years to Leroy, a descendant of one of the Founding Fathers of the USA, and they have seven children ranging in age from five to nineteen. Leroy is of pure Yankee stock but has opted out of all the proud Yankee traditions and the conventional rat-race by becoming a carpenter. He favours a simple, austere and Puritan lifestyle in opposition to the rampant materialism he sees around him. He even finds it hard to charge the going rate for his skills. However, this rigid austerity has been thrust on his family and the threat of poverty looms ever larger in their lives. Patricia's depression stems from a sense of deep disappointment with her life and a fear of what the future holds. She yearns for a more comfortable and affluent lifestyle, resenting the life she feels Leroy has imposed on her. She veers from elation to resentment. Now, for the first time in twenty years, she has weaned herself off anti-depressants but she cannot offer any reason why she has been able to do this. In this scene, as she confides in Karen, another patient in the hospital, she becomes increasingly agitated.

PATRICIA. I just don't know whether to tell him yet.
[KAREN. What?]
That I'm off everything.
[KAREN. But he'll like that, won't he?]
Oh yes. But he's going to be doubtful. – Which I am, too, let's face it – I've been on one medication or another for almost twenty years. But I do feel a thousand per cent better. And I really have no idea how it happened. (*Shakes her head.*) Dear God, when I think of him hanging-in there all

these years . . . I'm so ashamed. But at the same time he's absolutely refused to make any money, every one of our children has had to work since they could practically write their names. I can't be expected to applaud, exactly. (*Presses her eyes.*) I guess sooner or later you just have to stand up and say, 'I'm normal, I made it.' But it's like standing on top of a stairs and there's no stairs. (*Staring ahead.*)

[KAREN. I think I'd better go out to him. Should I tell your husband you're coming out?

PATRICIA. I think I'll wait a minute.

KAREN (*stands*). He seems very nice.]

– I'll tell you the truth, dear – I've put him through hell and I know it . . . (*Tears threaten her.*) I know I have to stop blaming him; it came to me like a visitation two weeks ago, I-must-not-blame-Leroy-anymore. And it's amazing, I lost all desire for medication, I could feel it leaving me like a . . . like a ghost. (*Slight pause.*) It's just that he's got really well-to-do relatives and he simply will not accept anyone's help. I mean you take the Jews, the Italians, Irish – they've got their Italian-Americans, Irish-Americans, Hispanic-Americans – they stick together and help each other. But you ever hear of Yankee-Americans? Not on your life. Raise his taxes, rob him blind, the Yankee'll just sit there all alone getting sadder and sadder. – But I'm not going to think about it anymore.

COMMENTARY: Patricia is in a quandary. The fact that she has been dependent on drugs for twenty years must have a major effect on how this monologue is delivered: 'It's like standing on top of a stairs and there's no stairs.' She struggles to find the words to express her confusion and anger as she confronts the real world which is no longer mediated for her by drugs. She's a lonely woman who resents feeling isolated and adrift. She's married to a loner but wants to be part of a group, part of the inviting world around her. Suddenly the floodgates open and all her feelings, repressed and bottled up over the years, begin to gush forth in this speech.

Laughing Wild
Christopher Durang

Act 1, scene 1. Nondescript 'limbo' setting.

Woman (30s) is 'dressed fairly normally. She sits in a chair and talks to the audience. She can get up from the chair from time to time if the spirit moves her'. The play opens with this monologue.

WOMAN. Oh, it's all such a mess. Look at this mess. My hair is a mess. My clothes are a mess.

I want to talk to you about life. It's just too difficult to be alive, isn't it, and to try to function? There are all these people to deal with. I tried to buy a can of tuna fish in the supermarket, and there was this *person* standing right in front of where I wanted to reach out to get the tuna fish, and I waited a while, to see if they'd move, and they didn't – they were looking at tuna fish too, but they were taking a real long time on it, reading the ingredients on each can like they were a book, a pretty boring book, if you ask me, but nobody has; so I waited a long while, and they didn't move, and I couldn't get to the tuna fish cans; and I thought about asking them to move, but then they seemed so stupid not to have *sensed* that I needed to get by them that I had this awful fear that it would do no good, no good at all, to ask them, they'd probably say something like, 'We'll move when we're goddam ready, you nagging bitch,' and then what would I do? And so then I started to cry out of frustration, quietly, so as not to disturb anyone, and still, even though I was softly sobbing, this stupid person didn't *grasp* that I needed to get by them to reach the goddam tuna fish, people are so insensitive, I just hate them, and so I reached over with my fist, and I brought it down real hard on his head and I screamed: 'Would you kindly move, asshole!!!'

And the person fell to the ground, and looked totally startled, and some child nearby started to cry, and I was still crying, and I couldn't imagine making use of the tuna fish now anyway, and so I shouted at the child to stop crying – I mean, it was drawing too much attention to me – and I ran out of the supermarket, and I thought, I'll take a taxi to the Metropolitan Museum of Art, I need to be surrounded with culture right now, not tuna fish.

COMMENTARY: As the play progresses it becomes clear that the Woman is a mental patient. The nature of her mania and obsessions become increasingly apparent in her ranting monologue which forms the first scene of the play. In this excerpt she seems articulate and coherent (though a bit extreme). You must not reveal too much of her madness at this point. She should appear almost sane, it's the other person in her version of events who must appear to be mad. In her warped mind she is always the victim as contemporary urban life conspires against her. Everywhere she goes she feels confronted by barriers and obstructions. She easily feels slighted and is always spoiling for a fight. For her the rest of the world is always to blame.

Lettice and Lovage
Peter Shaffer

Act 1, scene 2. The offices of the Preservation Trust in London.

Lettice Douffet (40s) 'is a lady in middle life'. She has a 'natural exuberance'. She works as a tour guide appointed by the Preservation Trust to show visitors around Fustian House, a Tudor mansion. Lettice has been summoned to Lotte Schoen's office to talk about her fitness to continue with her job. Lotte is concerned that 'reports have been coming in steadily for some time now of bizarre inaccuracies in your tour . . . Gross departures from fact and truth.' Lettice is the first to admit that she has scant regard for accuracy in her tour lectures, finding the true history of Fustian Hall far too dull. Instead she favours embellishing her talks with romantic flourishes and historical fictions. Lettice's mother, with her rallying cry of 'Enlarge! Enliven! Enlighten!' and her all-female touring theatre company devoted to performing Shakespeare in French, was a formidable influence. Lettice's livelihood depends on keeping this job and she approaches this interview with trepidation. 'She is wearing a black beret and a theatrical black cloak like some medieval abbot. She carries a leather satchel and is very uneasy.' In this speech she recounts the thrilling history of her mother's touring theatre company.

LETTICE. [Indeed.] My mother married a Free French soldier in London called Douffet, who abandoned her within three months of the wedding. She had no pleasure thereafter in associating with Frenchmen. 'They are all fickle,' she used to say. 'Fickle and furtive.'
[LOTTE: A fair description of the whole nation, I would say.]
She brought me up entirely by herself. Mainly on the road. We played all over the Dordogne – in farmhouses and barns, wherever they would have us. We performed only the

54

history plays of Shakespeare – because history was my mother's passion. I was the stage manager, responsible for costumes, props and historical detail. She herself was famous for her Richard III. She used to wear a pillow on her back as a hump. It was brilliantly effective. No one who heard it will ever forget the climax of her performance – the cry of total despair wrung from her on the battlefield: 'Un cheval! Un cheval! Mon royaume pour un cheval!' (LOTTE *stares, astounded*.) All the translations were her own.

[LOTTE (*drily*). A remarkable achievement.]

[Not for her.] Language was her other passion. As I grew up I was never permitted to read anything but the grandest prose. 'Language alone frees one,' she used to say. 'And History gives one place.' She was adamant I should not lose my English Heritage, either of words or deeds. Every night she enacted for me a story from our country's past – fleshing it out with her own marvellous virtuosity! Richard's battlefield with the crown hung up in the thornbush! King Charles the First going to his execution on a freezing January morning – putting on two shirts lest when he trembled from cold his enemies should think it was from fear! *Wonderful!* . . . On a child's mind the most tremendous events were engraved as with diamond on a window pane. And to me, my tourists – simply random holidaymakers in my care for twenty minutes of their lives – are *my* children in this respect. It is my duty to enlarge them. Enlarge – enliven – enlighten them.

COMMENTARY: So much of Lettice's speech is characterized by a grand and dramatic use of words. All learned, we find out, from being on the road with her actress mother and watching her, night after night, from the wings. She picks her words for effect (the 'fickle and furtive' French). She's also been indoctrinated by an influential parent to feel that the dissemination of history and English heritage is a kind of didactic mission to be taken to the masses. Lettice is a character full of zeal and totally lacking in doubts. Her entire speech has the confident build of a soliloquy from a Shakespearean history play. She knows exactly where she is taking her audience. She's also an excellent actress with impeccable timing.

The Love Space Demands
Ntozake Shange

'Serial Monogamy'

'The Love Space Demands' is a 'choreopoem' reflecting the lives of African-American women. Each poem is structured as a monologue, focusing on the problems of race, gender and sex. This monologue examines the possibilities and consequences of lust and love, of infatuations and intimacy.

i think/we should reexamine/serial monogamy
is it/one at a time or
one for a long time?
      how
does the concept of infinity relate to a skilled
serial monogamist/& can
that person consider a diversionary escapade
a serial
one night stand?
      can a consistent
serial monogamist
have one/several/or myriad relationships
that broach every pore of one's body
 so long as there is no penetration?
do we/consider adventurous relentless tongues
capable of penetration & if we do
can said tongues whip thru us indiscriminately
with words/like

    'hello'
 'oh, you lookin good'

'you jigglin, baby'
cd these be reckless immature violations of
serial monogamy?

   i mean/
if my eyes light up cuz
   some stranger just lets go/caint stop hisself
from sayin
            'yr name must be paradise'
   if i was to grin or tingle/even get a lil happy/
hearin me & paradise/
      now synonyms
does that make me a scarlet woman?
      if i wear a red dress that makes someone else hot
      does that put me out the fryin pan & into the
fire?

say/
my jade bracelet got hot
                  (which aint possible cuz jade aint
jade
            if it aint cold)
but say
my jade got lit up & burst offa my wrist
& i say/
         'i gotta find my precious stones
cuz they my luck'
                  & he say
'luck don't leave it goes where
you need it'
            & i say
'i gotta find my bracelet'
            & he say
'you know for actual truth
                  you was wearin this bracelet?'

& i say
  'a course, it's my luck'
                  & he say
'how you know?'
& i say
        'cuz
        i heard my jade
        flyin thru the air
        over yr head
        behind my knees
        &
        up under the Japanese lampshade!'
              & he say
'you heard yr jade flyin thru the air?'
        'yes'
              i say
'& where were they flyin from'
          he say
        'from my arm' i say
        'they got hot & jumped offa my arm'
'but/
where was yr arm?'
            he say
& i caint say mucha nothin
cuz
where my arm was a part a some tremendous
current/
cd be 'lectricity or niggahs on fire/
so where my arm was is where/jade gets hot
& does that imply the failure of serial monogamy?

do flamin flyin jade stones
on a arm/that is a kiss/& a man who knows where/
luck is
take the serial/outta monogamy/& leave
love?

COMMENTARY: This poem demands to be performed. But like any poem spoken aloud it should not sound like verse but normal speech. It begins like a lecture and then transforms into a flashy, surreal performance piece, all hot and 'lectric. The sections of 'i say' and 'he say' turn the piece into a duet, allowing you to control the fantasy notion of jade flying in every direction. One of the special properties of the speech is its rich use of colour, texture and light. It drifts away from the subject (serial monogamy) and takes unexpected flight into another realm of experience.

Low Level Panic
Clare McIntyre

Scene 1. A bathroom. A sunny summer morning.

Jo (20s) shares a flat with two other girls. She is taking a bath and chatting to her flatmate Mary. They have been talking about the pornographic magazine which Mary found 'in the bin'. Jo is self-absorbed and very concerned that she is too fat, too short, too spotty and that she has an 'unattractive clitoris'. But she is self-deprecating in an amusing way. In this speech Jo reveals her fantasy of being 'an astonishingly beautiful, mysterious, fascinating woman'.

JO *stretches both her legs vertically out of the bath and looks at them.*
JO. What do you think?
[MARY. What?]
My legs?
[MARY. What about them?]
They look really good.
[MARY. Why?]
Like this.
[MARY. Do they?
I think so.
MARY. They don't look any different.]
Course they do. Don't you look at pictures of yourself upside down?
[MARY. No.]
I look amazing.
[MARY. You're obsessed.]
If I could grow six inches and be as fat as I am now I'd be really tall and thin. I could stretch out all the fat on my legs

61

till they were long and slender and I'd go to swanky bars and smoke menthol cigarettes and I'd wrap my new legs round cocktail stools and I'd smooth myself all over with my delicate hands and I'd have my hair up so you could see my neck. I'd save all the pennies I see lying about on the streets in an old whisky bottle then I'd go out and buy silky underwear with lots of lace on it and suspenders and that's what I'd wear. I wouldn't wear anything else because that would spoil it. I'd wear that and a lot of make-up and I'd snake my way around bars and hotels in Mayfair and I'd be able to drink whatever I like. I'd have cocktails and white wine out of bottles with special dates on them in tall glasses that were all dewy with cold and I'd smile a lot. I wouldn't laugh. I wouldn't guffaw. I'd just smile and show my teeth and I'd really be somebody then.

COMMENTARY: This is a fantasy speech delivered with unembarrassed freedom. It's about looking at yourself from a completely different angle and seeing a whole new you. Like *Alice in Wonderland*, a sudden shift in height leads to an outrageous chain reaction. The body snaps into shape and suddenly it all fits together into one shapely, sexy mass. The speech also suggests a whole new freedom of movement. Suddenly places denied to you open their doors. And you don't have to do anything at all to make it happen. It just falls into place. Every word in the speech is very specific, each event is very calculated.

The Madness of Esme and Shaz
Sarah Daniels

Scene 7. A city park.

Shaz (33) has spent thirteen years in Broadmoor Prison serving a sentence for murder. As a child she had been taken into special care because her father sexually abused her. Her release is approved but it is conditional on 'care' being arranged for her outside. The Social Services track down Shaz's Aunt, Esme, who was estranged from her brother so she never even realized that she had a niece. She agrees to take Shaz in although they are an unlikely pair: Esme is an unmarried, retired civil servant and a devout Christian. Shaz is feisty, confrontational and speaks her mind. Shaz's only interests are TV and music, and for the past thirteen years they provided her only connection with the world outside. Quickly upon her release Shaz starts up a lesbian relationship with Pat, who is studying for a Ph.D. and working as a ticket conductor on British Rail. This scene takes place ten weeks after they have met. Shaz has avoided telling Pat about herself, but when Pat invites her to live with her Shaz decides to reveal all. Pat wrongly assumes that Shaz killed her father and in this speech Shaz puts the record straight.

SHAZ (*without emotion*). Three years after I was taken into care my Mother died. I didn't feel anything. I thought. 'That's it then. My Mother's dead.' She'd not visited me in three years. I was in care because she put him before me.
[PAT. Women's conditioning is so strong.]
(*Without looking at her.*) You won't find any easy answers for this in the books you've read.
[PAT. I'm sorry. Go on.]
But when she died a feeling of hope went. Anyway several years later my Father married again. They had two children a boy, and a baby girl. I left care when I was sixteen. You

63

had to. I got a job in an old peoples home. I was – . Oh. I don't know. My behaviour was rather strange. I used to cut myself. No one ever knew. They told me I was very good at my job. They had no idea. I was – it was like I was very cut off. I decided to look for and found my Father. He was pleased enough to be reunited. I baby-sat for them. They gave me a key to the house. Sometimes when I knew they were out I would let myself in and write stuff with her lipstick over the mirror. Tip her perfume over the bed. Smear body lotion into the carpet. One evening I was babysitting. (*She stops.*)

[PAT. You, you killed the little boy?]

[No.] I murdered the baby. Girl. I picked her up from her crib thing and held her. Squeezed her. Until she stopped breathing. When I knew she was dead, I sat down, turned the telly up and waited for them to come home.

COMMENTARY: The speech is constructed in such a way as to build tension slowly and then release it through the details of a horrible event. Shaz is lost from the very beginning of the play. She's been abandoned, 'cut-off' to feelings. The father divided her from her mother – a crucial bit of knowledge. Here she is opening up and revealing herself. The horror of her act is made all the more chilling because of the economy of both details and emotion in her matter-of-fact confession. The speech is delivered very straight and without any melodramatic flourish.

Man to Man
Manfred Karge (translated by Anthony Vivis)

Scene 5. Germany.

Ella/Max Gericke (no age given) is a manual worker. The play is set between 1930 and the present day. Ella is an ordinary working class woman in the 1930s who marries Max. But as her situation worsens during the Weimar Republic and then under Hitler, she is forced to take the extreme measure of assuming the clothes and identity of her dead husband. In this speech she describes this transformation.

ELLA/MAX. My first man was a volunteer from Saxony
A chronic drunk and brilliant with it.
He ran from hole to hole and over bodies dead and dying
And used me as a transit camp *en route*.
My second fella was my big romance.
We loved each other madly, as they say.
But he got drowned before the wedding.
I really was unlucky with my men.

By nineteen I was married. My Dad said: Well, you can wave goodbye to youth and innocence, and all that's special and unique. My marriage lasted one year, seven months, and twelve days. My husband was a crane-operator with Nagel and Sons. He wasn't a bad sort, and he did have a job. I'd heard about that before I'd heard his name. I did find out his name later though, but what I didn't know was that the sciatica, which'd been bothering him for years, was cancer. We got to know each other in a country restaurant. He drank beer. I drank *Weisse mit Schuss*. He took me back to his room. His chair was his wardrobe, so I had to sit on the bed. He kneeled at my feet and unbuttoned my blouse.

So this is what paradise is like, I thought to myself, and said: I love you. You don't have to overdo it, he said, but I said it again: I love you. And when we'd slept together he said: No tits, your arse too tight, you look to me like fucking Snow White. I had to laugh. And then he tried to write Snow White on my wet belly. His finger was all yellow from too much smoking. Even now, whenever I hear anyone say Snow White I come over all peculiar. But we wasn't to be happy for long. So as not to lose his job, Max kept on going to work day after day, illness or no illness, but hardly ever bothered to see the doctor. The sodding sciatica was making his life hell.

His hand, now boneless, manages once again
To operate the gear-stick and controls,
To unwrap his bread and dripping, lift a cup,
Pull his cap right down over his face
To hide his yellow cheeks, and open up
His shirt, to give that sweat-soaked body
A breath of air; but Daddy Cancer
Sends his daughters on the rampage,
And feeds them Max's last remaining bones, and joints, and
    veins.
So now from sleep to sleep
From one day's work to another
With only his braces holding him together
He drags the half-eaten shell his body has become.
A ray of hope lights up the gloom:
His hand can raise a glass and stroke
His wife's behind, but soon
His hands go, his legs, and then his head and belly.
His body starts to shrivel up. Snow White
Acquires a dwarf.

At work, the guy Max had most contact with was called
Erwin – his trousers always had a razor-sharp crease and his

nickname was The Best Dressed Man in Mecklenburg. So, when I'd made up mind that come what may I'd take over my husband's job as a crane-operator at Nagel and Sons, it was Erwin I was most afraid would recognise me. So I cut off my hair and altered my husband's clothes and then, to help me through the first few days, I pretended I'd fallen downstairs. I hoped that by winding bandages round my head, by wearing a sort of disguise, if you like, my work-mates would gradually get used to the new face of Max Gericke. It was risky but I had no choice. I think I must've started planning it before my husband died, because, without knowing why, and much to his amazement, I had got him to explain how everything in the control cabin worked, and describe it down to the last detail. Against all expectation, I was able to carry out my plan quite easily, mainly because while he was working away up there in the control cabin my late lamented husband hardly ever spoke to any of his mates. Except for The Best Dressed Man in Mecklenburg, who used to scurry up the ladder every now and again to get away from a sticky situation down below. Beggars can't be choosers, and apart from the odd minor cock-up manoeuvring crates around, which the others put down to my accident, I did bloody well. Unfortunately, as a result of these extraordinary events, my dear departed ended up getting a cut-price funeral in some provincial town, with his widow's name carved on the gravestone. Here lies Ella Gericke, born in Frankfurt-an-der-Oder, died of cancer. R.I.P. Jesus Christ, the nerve of the woman.

And on the third day he rose again from the dead.
I had to rise the next day at five a.m.
I, my own widow, my late lamented husband, had to be
Man enough to wear the fucking trousers.
Why was being a woman not enough?

COMMENTARY: The dramatist gives minimal stage directions and no descriptions of his characters. This gives the actor maximum freedom to interpret the role and relate the narrative to her own particular experience. The writing is spare and austere, combining poetic (verse) and naturalistic (prose) sequences. The material is based on a factual case. The monologue is full of remarkable events (the 'Snow White' sections) and turns banal details into the stuff of poetic elegy. There are lots of mechanistic, male images in the speech which the female character has to reconcile herself to and work with. All the details are told matter-of-factly and coolly as though we are witnessing a curious evolutionary process in which a woman gradually assumes the identity of her dead husband. Throughout the speech Ella is recreating and revealing her identity and sexuality.

Molly Sweeney
Brian Friel

Act 1.

Molly Sweeney (41) has been blind since she was ten months old. She was 'an only child. Father a judge. Mother in and out of institutions all her days with nervous trouble. Brought up by various housekeepers. For some reason she had never been sent to a school for the blind. Said she didn't know why . . . She wasn't totally sightless: she could distinguish between light and dark . . . But for all practical purposes she had no useful sight.' The author gives this note for the actor: 'Most people with impaired vision look and behave like fully-sighted people. The only evidence of their disability is usually a certain vacancy in the eyes or the way the head is held. Molly should indicate her disability in some such subtle way. No canes, no groping, no dark glasses, etc.' There is no self-pity or sense of resignation when she speaks of her disability. She works as a massage therapist at a local health club and this was where she met Frank Sweeney, her husband of two years. They married only one month after first meeting each other. Frank, who is unemployed and a dreamer, persuades her to visit an eye surgeon in the hope that he will restore her sight. She however is completely content with her life and finds great joy in her work and recreation (especially swimming). This speech opens the play.

MOLLY. By the time I was five years of age, my father had taught me the names of dozens of flowers and herbs and shrubs and trees. He was a judge and his work took him all over the county. And every evening, when he got home, after he'd had a few quick drinks, he'd pick me up in his arms and carry me out to the walled garden.

'Tell me now,' he'd ask. 'Where precisely are we?'

'We're in your garden.'

69

'Oh, you're such a clever little missy!' And he'd pretend to smack me.

'Exactly what part of my garden?'

'We're beside the stream.'

'Stream? Do you hear a stream? I don't. Try again.'

'We're under the lime tree.'

'I smell no lime tree. Sorry. Try again.'

'We're beside the sundial.'

'You're guessing. But you're right. And at the bottom of the pedestal there is a circle of petunias. There are about twenty of them all huddled together in one bed. They are – what? – seven inches tall. Some of them are blue-and-white, and some of them are pink, and a few have big, red, cheeky faces. Touch them.'

And he would bend over, holding me almost upside down, and I would have to count them and smell them and feel their velvet leaves and their sticky stems. Then he'd test me.

'Now, Molly. Tell me what you saw.'

'Petunias.'

'How many petunias did you see?'

'Twenty.'

'Colour?'

'Blue-and-white and pink and red.'

'Good. And what shape is their bed?'

'It's a circle.'

'Splendid. Passed with flying colours. You *are* a clever lady.'

And to have got it right for him and to hear the delight in his voice gave me such pleasure.

Then we'd move on to his herb bed and to his rose bed and to his ageratum and his irises and his azaleas and his sedum. And when we'd come to his nemophila, he always said the same thing.

'Nemophila are sometimes called Baby Blue Eyes. I know

you can't see them but they have beautiful blue eyes. Just like you. You're my nemophila.'

And then we'd move on to the shrubs and the trees and we'd perform the same ritual of naming and counting and touching and smelling. Then, when our tour was ended, he'd kiss my right cheek and then my left cheek with that old-world formality with which he did everything; and I loved that because his whiskey breath made my head giddy for a second.

'Excellent!' he'd say. 'Excellent testimony! We'll adjourn until tomorrow.'

Then if Mother were away in hospital with her nerves, he and I would make our own meal. But if she were at home she'd appear at the front door – always in her headscarf and wellingtons – and she'd shout, 'Molly! Daddy! Dinner!' I never heard her call him anything but Daddy and the word always seemed to have a mocking edge. And he'd say to me, 'Even scholars must eat. Let us join your mother.'

And sometimes, just before we'd go into that huge, echoing house, sometimes he'd hug me to him and press his mouth against my ear and whisper with fierce urgency, 'I promise you, my darling, you aren't missing a lot; not a lot at all. Trust me.'

Of course I trusted him; completely. But late at night, listening to Mother and himself fighting their weary war downstairs and then hearing him grope his way unsteadily to bed, I'd wonder what he meant. And it was only when I was about the same age as he was then, it was only then that I thought – I thought perhaps I was beginning to understand what he meant. But that was many, many years later. And by then Mother and he were long dead and the old echoing house was gone. And I had been married to Frank for over two years. And by then, too, I had had the operation on the first eye.

COMMENTARY: The speech is full of memories and atmosphere. The voices and conversations of the past are echoed by Molly. She remembers everything in great detail: the smell, shapes and textures of her father's garden which she experienced through her other senses. Though she cannot see she manages to filter in the world around her through language. Molly has a particularly acute sense of hearing and monitors everything that is said. Her life is one continuous narrative in which someone – her father, for instance, or Frank – pick up the thread. She's a very peaceful character, almost religious in her tranquillity. But she is always in danger of having someone else's vision and opinions imposed on her. So the world and those around her do pose threats to her independence and integrity.

Moonlight
Harold Pinter

One Act. A bedroom where Jake and Fred are talking.

*Maria (50), who is married to Ralph, is a friend of Jake and Fred's
parents. The boys also have a sister named Bridget. This is Maria's first
appearance in the play and she enters to talk to the two sons of a dying
man named Andy. She is a close friend of their mother Bel. Why she
enters at this moment is a complete mystery. Nothing about her has been
mentioned before nor is she described in any great detail in the play.*

MARIA. Do you remember me? I was your mother's best
friend. You're both so tall. I remember you when you were
little boys. And Bridget of course. I once took you all to the
Zoo, with your father. We had tea. Do you remember? I
used to come to tea, with your mother. We drank so much
tea in those days! My three are all in terribly good form.
Sarah's doing marvellously well and Lucien's thriving at the
Consulate and as for Susannah, there's no stopping her. But
don't you remember the word games we all used to play?
Then we'd walk across the Common. That's where we met
Ralph. He was refereeing a football match. He did it, oh I
don't know, with such aplomb, such command. Your
mother and I were so . . . impressed. He was always ahead
of the game. He knew where the ball was going before it was
kicked. Osmosis. I think that's the word. He's still as
osmotic as anyone I've ever come across. Much more so, of
course. Most people have no osmotic quality whatsoever.
But of course in those days – I won't deny it – I had a great
affection for your father. And so had your mother – for your
father. Your father possessed little in the way of osmosis but

73

nor did he hide his blushes under a barrel. I mean he wasn't a pretender, he didn't waste precious time. And how he danced. How he danced. One of the great waltzers. An elegance and grace long gone. A firmness and authority so seldom encountered. And he looked you directly in the eye. Unwavering. As he swirled you across the floor. A rare gift. But I was young in those days. So was your mother. Your mother was marvellously young and quickening every moment. I – I must say – particularly when I saw your mother being swirled across the floor by your father – felt buds breaking out all over the place. I thought I'd go mad.

COMMENTARY: This is a memory speech. It has the freedom of a dream. In the pattern of the play characters suddenly appear from nowhere without any introduction. The speech hides details. There are seven characters and their lives are crucially linked to one another. Maria and the boys' father Andy have had a love affair that went on for many years. Maria has also had a sexual relationship with their mother Bel. There is much talk of hidden passions and lust throughout the play. But clarity is always kept veiled. Maria's speech seems to disclose that the relationships with Andy and Bel were going on during the boys' childhood (she went to the zoo with the father and came to tea with the mother). Unlike Jake and Fred, who act like dysfunctional young men, Maria's children are thriving; a perfect family unit. The speech is full of good cheer which Maria maintains throughout the play. There is no sense whatsoever that other people have been hurt by her actions. She remembers the past as a golden time full of tea drinking and waltzing.

My Mother Said I Never Should
Charlotte Keatley

Act 3, scene 5. The garden of Ken and Margaret's suburban semi in Rayne's Park, London, late May 1987, early morning.

Jackie Metcalfe (34) runs her own art gallery in Manchester. At the age of nineteen she had an illegitimate baby. When the baby, Rosie, was three months old, Jackie found that she couldn't cope with the demands of single parenthood. So she handed Rosie over to her mother and father, Margaret and Ken, to raise as if she were their own daughter. She makes sure that Rosie only knows her as her own sister, but she always feels the strain of the pretence. Jackie visits her parents and Rosie from time to time as her career and travels allow. When Rosie is fifteen and on holiday with Jackie in Italy, Rosie asks if she can come and live with her in Manchester. Jackie agrees. Margaret takes this news badly. She is resentful that Jackie comes along like a fairy to whisk Rosie away. It turns out that Margaret has stomach cancer and Jackie and Rosie come down from Manchester to visit her in hospital. The night that Jackie flies back to Manchester for an opening at her gallery, Margaret dies. This emotional scene takes place only two hours after Margaret's death. Ken and Rosie come home to sort through the relevant family birth and marriage certificates. It is while doing this that Rosie finally discovers that it is Jackie, not Margaret, who is her true mother. When Jackie returns from Manchester Rosie angrily confronts her 'mother' and Jackie responds with this speech.

JACKIE. I wanted you to have opportunities I couldn't ever have given you.
[ROSIE. No you didn't. You wanted your own life more than you wanted mine!
JACKIE. Don't!
ROSIE. If you were really my Mum you wouldn't have been able to give me away!

75

JACKIE. How dare you! (*Goes to hit* ROSIE *but cannot.*)]
You're at the centre of everything I do! (*Slight pause.*)
Mummy treated me as though I'd simply fallen over and cut
my knee, – picked me up and said you'll be all right now, it
won't show much. She wanted to make it all better. (*Quiet.*)
. . . She was the one who wanted it kept secret . . . I
WANTED you, Rosie. (*Angry.*) For the first time in my life
I took care of myself – refused joints, did exercises, went to
the clinic. (*Pause.*) 'It's a girl'. (*Smiles irresistibly.*) – After
you'd gone I tried to lose that memory. (*Pause. Effort.*)
Graham . . . your Father. (*Silence.*) He couldn't be there the
day you were born, he had to be in Liverpool. He was
married. (*Emphatic.*) He loved me, he loved you, you must
believe that! (*Pause.*) He said he'd leave his wife, but I knew
he wouldn't; there were two children, the youngest was only
four . . . we'd agreed, separate lives, I wanted to bring you
up. He sent money. (*Pause.*) I took you to Lyme Park one
day, I saw them together, across the lake, he was buying
them ice creams, his wife was taking a photo. I think they
live in Leeds now, I saw his name in the Guardian last year,
an article about his photographs . . . (*Pause.*) It was a very
cold winter after you were born. There were power cuts. I
couldn't keep the room warm; there were no lights in the
tower blocks; I knew he had an open fire, it was trendy; so
we took a bus to Didsbury, big gardens, pine kitchens, made
a change from concrete. I rang the bell. (*Stops.*) A Punjabi
man answered, said he was sorry . . . they'd moved. By the
time we got back to Mosside it was dark, the lift wasn't
working – (*Stops.*) That was the night I phoned Mummy.
(*Difficult.*) Asked her. (*Pause.*) I tried! I couldn't do it,
Rosie. (*Pause.*) It doesn't matter how much you succeed
afterwards, if you've failed once. (*Pause.*) After you'd gone
. . . I kept waking in the night to feed you . . . A week . . .
in the flat . . . Then I went back to art school. Sandra and
Hugh thought I was inhuman. I remember the books that
came out that winter – how to succeed as a single working

mother – fairytales! (*Pause*.) Sandra and Hugh have a family now. Quite a few of my friends do. (*Pause*.) I could give you everything now. Rosie? . . .

COMMENTARY: Jackie's thoughts unfold in quick snapshots, almost as if she can only flash brief images of the past before her daughter's eyes. She's groping for justification and reconciliation, hoping that she'll be forgiven if she lays out the facts and circumstances, stressing the pressures and demands from her point of view. Jackie's feeling of guilt and grief at this moment must be enormous. She has lost her mother and is on the verge of losing her daughter. At the centre of the speech is a dark, cold core: the decision Jackie took to surrender her daughter. Throughout the monologue Jackie throws up images of a lonely, terrified woman traveling from place to place in search of warmth and safety. Notice how childlike and selfish her tone is. She wants to forget the mess of the past and focus on 'now'. She is begging Rosie for a second chance.

Oleanna
David Mamet

Act 3. John's office in an American college.

Carol (20) is a student. She is halfway through one of her courses, taught by John, and is in a panic. She fears she is failing the course because she has understood nothing. She comes to John for help and tries to explain her problem, 'I'm smiling in class, I'm smiling the whole time. What are you talking about? What is everyone talking about? I don't understand. I don't know what it means. I don't know what it means to be here.' John tries to reassure her, mentioning his own youthful uncertainties, cracking off-colour jokes and generally lambasting the whole notion of higher education. He ends by putting a consoling hand on her shoulder. In consultation with her 'group' she decides all this is grounds for claiming sexual harassment and she sends a letter to the committee considering John's application to become a tenured member of the college faculty. John is appalled by this accusation and refuses to believe it. He is worried not only about the professional implications but also about financial ones as he is in the process of buying a new house. In contrast, as Carol moves ahead with her accusation her muddled despair transforms into an iron-willed certainty. In this scene John, having been suspended, is making one last desperate attempt to save his reputation. He has asked Carol to come to his office and is trying to persuade her to retract the accusation and 'forgive' him. This speech is her response to him.

CAROL. [Then *say* it.] For Christ's sake. Who the *hell* do you think that you are? You want a post. You want unlimited power. To do and to say what you want. As it pleases you – Testing, Questioning, Flirting . . .
[JOHN. I never . . .]
Excuse me, one moment, will you? (*She reads from her notes.*)
   The twelfth: 'Have a good day, dear.'

The fifteenth: 'Now, don't *you* look fetching . . .'

April seventeenth: 'If you girls would come over here . . .' I saw you. I saw you, Professor. For two semesters sit there, stand there and exploit our, as you thought, 'paternal prerogative', and what is that but rape; I swear to God. You asked me in here to explain something to me, as a child, that I did not understand. But I came to explain something to you. You Are Not God. You ask me why I came? I came here to instruct you. (*She produces his book.*)

And your book? You think you're going to show me some 'light'? You '*maverick.*' Outside of tradition. No, no, (*She reads from the book's liner notes.*) '*of* that fine tradition of *inquiry.* Of Polite *skepticism*' . . . and you say you believe in free intellectual discourse. YOU BELIEVE IN NOTHING. YOU BELIEVE IN NOTHING AT ALL.

COMMENTARY: The entire action of *Oleanna* is a battle of wills with the balance of power shifting away from John and towards Carol. She begins the play in a weak and vulnerable position. Early on she was silent, now she is eloquent with accusatory rhetoric. The student has turned teacher. The actress playing Carol must decide where her strength comes from at this late stage in the drama. Could it come from her new-found sense of articulacy and confidence? Could it be fear and hatred of John's paternalistic maleness? The play is never explicit on these points and the actor must fill in the blanks. Carol's anger never subsides but only becomes more manifest. No longer alone, she has the backing of a group of female supporters who have helped provide her with a language. She has become a fervent zealot. Her zeal moves her to destroy John.

The Pitchfork Disney
Philip Ridley

One 1. A dimly lit room in the East End of London. Night.

Haley Stray (28) lives with her twin brother, Presley. They are both chocaholics; their addiction is so exteme that they survive solely on a diet of chocolate. Haley is 'wearing an old nightdress beneath a man's frayed dressing gown. Her hair is unevenly hacked. Her teeth discoloured, skin pale, dark rings beneath bloodshot eyes.' Their parents mysteriously 'disappeared' ten years ago, and they maintain a connection with them by rationing their parents' medicine which was left behind. Always in a state of terror and dread, they experience the world as a living nightmare. Macabre and bizarre fantasy defines their existence. Although they are in their late twenties they regress and behave like children: it is as if the clock stopped for them when they were ten years old. They are like children in a fairy tale: innocents threatened by an evil (in this case nuclear) world. They live hermetically together in a fortified home, shunning all contact with the outside. Presley dominates their relationship, intimidating Haley by rationing the medicine and tranquilizers to keep her docile. Presley is the historian of their comforting, golden childhood and Haley relies on him to recount key episodes. In this speech Haley is telling Presley about her last traumatic trip to the shops.

HALEY. Don't blame me. You remember what happened last time I went to the shops. It was terrible. I was so scared. I came back crying and shaking. My clothes were torn and wet. There was blood on my legs. You wiped it away with a tissue. I was crying so much I couldn't breathe properly. You remember that, Presley? I was hysterical. Wasn't I? Hysterical?
[PRESLEY (*softly*). I suppose so.]

You were so nice. You put your arms round me and let me suck the dummy. You remember that?

[PRESLEY. Yes.]

And I told you what happened. How when I got to the end of the street a pack of dogs appeared. Seven of them. Big, filthy dogs. With maggots in their fur. Foam on their lips. Eyes like clots of blood. One dog started to sniff me. Its nose was like an ice cube between my legs. Then it started to growl. Lips pulled back over yellow teeth. It started to chase me. I was running. Running and screaming. The other dogs chased me as well. All of them howling and snarling like wolves. They chased me over the wasteground. I fell. Fell into a pile of tin cans. There was a dead cat. My hand went into its stomach. All mushy like rotten fruit. I was screaming. Screaming so loud my throat tasted like blood. One of the dogs bit my coat. I pulled it away. The coat ripped. I ran and ran. All I could hear was snarling and growling and the sound of my own heart. I ran out of the wasteground. Through the old car park and into the derelict church. And still the dogs chased me. There I was, standing at the altar, with seven rabid animals coming down the aisles towards me. I picked up some old bibles and threw them. Did no good. The dogs ripped the bibles to pieces. I was so afraid. And the dogs could smell it. My fear. They were attracted by it. They came closer and closer and closer. I could feel their breath against my skin. Hot and reeking of vomit. I backed away. Stumbled up some steps. I wanted to pray. But I couldn't. I knew that if I could pray or sing a hymn, then the dogs would leave me alone. But all I could do was scream. Then one of the dogs made a lunge for me. I jumped up. Reached above me. Caught hold of something. It was smooth. Cool. Solid. I started to climb. Like climbing a tree. And I was halfway up before I realised I was climbing the marble crucifix and my chest was pressed close to the chest of Christ. It felt so comforting and safe. Then a dog bit at my feet. Pulled my shoe off. My toes were bleeding. A drop of

81

blood landed in the open mouth of the dog. It went berserk. Started to climb the crucifix. I scarpered higher, wrapped my legs round the waist of our Saviour, clung onto the crown of thorns for all I was worth. Then the base of the crucifix started to crumble. It rocked from side to side. Any minute it might fall and send me into the pack of dogs. Like a Christian to the hungry lions. I was so scared. So I kissed the lips of Christ. I said, 'Save me. Don't let the crucifix fall'. But the crucifix fell just the same. I crashed to the floor. The dogs nibbled at my bloodied fingers. I'm going to be eaten alive, I thought. Eaten by savage dogs. I screamed, 'Help me! Help me!'. And then . . . gun shots! I flinch at every one. I look round. The seven dogs are dead. Blood oozing from holes in their skulls. I feel sick. A Priest approaches me. He is holding a rifle. He asks me if I'm all right. I tell him I am. He says, 'Did you come for confession?'. And I say, 'Yes.' Because I think that's what he wants to hear and I owe him something for saving my life. So I go into confession with him and he asks me what I've done wrong. I tell him I can't think of anything. He says, 'Don't be stupid. No one's perfect'. I know he's right. I know there's something I've done. Something that made me a naughty girl once. But I can't think of what it is. I tell him I can't think of anything. He tells me to think harder. I can feel him getting angry and frustrated. He wants to forgive me but I'm not giving him the chance. Finally, I say, 'I kissed the lips of Christ and they tasted of chocolate'. He calls me a sinner and says I must repent. I ask him if I can be forgiven and he says, 'No! Your sins are too big'. I'm crying when I leave the church. I vow never to go shopping again.

COMMENTARY: Though adults, both Haley and her brother act like half-crazed, abandoned children. They live in fear of the unknown and the world outside. A trip to the shops is a perilous journey into the wild. The childhood trauma they appear to have suffered is never made entirely clear. But everything Haley says here reeks of absolute terror. It all sounds like a terrible nightmare come to life as a horror film. Yet all the surreal details are so vivid that the actress has to relive the incidents fully in order to make it work (e.g. being chased by the dogs). Much of the speech has Haley climbing higher and higher in an act of desperate escape. Even the refuge she finally finds from the priest leads to another off-balancing experience. It is clear that Haley has no safety in her life except her brother.

The Ride Down Mount Morgan
Arthur Miller

Act 1. A ward in Clearhaven Memorial Hospital in upstate New York.

Leah Felt (30), 'blondined hair, in an open raccoon coat, high heels', is married to Lyman Felt. They live together with their nine-year-old son, Benjamin, on a farm in upstate New York. Before meeting Lyman, Leah had had a successful career in the insurance business. Lyman has been in an accident while driving his Porsche down Mount Morgan. How he came to be driving down the mountain under treacherous conditions remains a mystery. He is bedridden, having broken multiple bones, and Leah has been summoned to his bedside. When she arrives at the hospital she finds that another Mrs Felt is already there with her grown-up daughter. It is an appalling revelation when both the Mrs Felts realize that they have been married to the same man. When Leah married Lyman he assured her that he had divorced his first wife, Theo. But it turns out that for the nine years preceding the accident Lyman had maintained the double life of a bigamist. In this scene Leah is confiding in Tom who, although a family friend, is also the lawyer for both Lyman and Theo.

LEAH (*slight pause*). – I could never take him back, but all this reminds me of an idea I used to have about him that . . . well, it'll sound mystical and silly . . .
[TOM. Please. I'd love to understand him.]
Well . . . it's that he *wants* so much; like a kid at a fair; a jelly apple here, a cotton candy there, and then a ride on a loop-the-loop . . . and it never lets up in him; and sometimes it almost seemed as though he'd lived once before, another life that was completely deprived, and this time around he mustn't miss a single thing. And that's what's so attractive about him – to women, I mean – Lyman's mind is up your

84

skirt but it's such a rare thing to be wanted like that – indifference is what most men feel now – I mean they have appetite but not hunger – and here is such a splendidly hungry man and it's simply . . . well . . . precious once you're past twenty-five. I tell you the truth, somewhere deep down I think I sensed something about him wasn't on the level, but . . . I guess I must have loved him so much that I . . . (*Breaks off.*) – But I mustn't talk this way; he's unforgiveable! It's the rottenest thing I've ever heard of! The answer is no, absolutely not!

COMMENTARY: There's a crucial balance in this speech between love and hate, acceptance and rejection. Lyman has had an indelible physical effect on Leah. He lives somewhere inside her. In the speech she gives herself over to this urge but then swiftly cuts-off and changes direction near the end. Leah has raw, animal urges which flash throughout the play. That side of her nature must be on display here before she closes down and denies Lyman at the end.

The Rise and Fall of Little Voice
Jim Cartwright

Act 1. A living-room, kitchen attached, open plan in a house in a Northern English Town.

Mari Hoff (40s) is a widow and lives with her daughter LV (short for Little Voice). She has no interest in being either a mother or a housewife and she dominates the painfully shy and agoraphobic LV with her crude, raunchy energy. Just beneath the surface of her blowsy and boozy exterior is a vivacious vulgarian. She is always on the prowl for a good lay and will flirt with anything in pants. For a night on the town she lacquers her hair, dons a revealing miniskirt and totters off in her high heels. All women to Mari, including LV, are rivals. In this scene she is talking to the monosyllabic Sadie, her next door neighbour, who is apparently her only friend and confidante, about her latest boyfriend, Ray Say.

MARI. Well, Sadie, what a night! What-a-night! What a championship neet! In fact come here and belt me. Calm me down with a smack sandwich so I can tell the tale. Belt me. (SADIE *comes over and hits* MARI's *two cheeks simultaneously.*) Tar. Well, I copped off again with that Ray. I did it again. He had no choice. You couldn't have got a bar between us last night, I became his side. I was eye to eye with him all night. There was virtually only enough virtual room to move our drinks table to gob. The turn was a romantic singer, thank fuck, and the music was in our heads, in our heads and in his wandering hands. Everyone's coming up to Ray allt' time, 'Howdo', 'Alright'. He knows so many people and I'm on his arm and his hands on my arse as he speaks to them. My arse. My golden old arse in Ray Say's hands. You can see how I am there. A queen. Queen for the night. He motored me home about a million miles an hour. I don't know what kinda car it is. One o'them big ones that bloody go, pistols in the back, all that, toaster in the dashboard, lights blinking on and off, put me up, put me down, put me up, put me down seats, thick as beds. Crack oh round the bloody roads we was. Heart in mouth, hand on leg, the lot. Then screeching to a halt outside, did you not hear us? You must be dead if you didn't. I saw every other curtain in the bitching road twitch. Then he comes at me with this pronto snog, lip-lapping like hell. That's men for you in it Sade, if you can remember. Lip-a-lapping, like old hell he was. But at least he's a lot better than most, at least he knows how to slide and dart and take a throat. At least there's always the thick wad of his wallet up against your tit for comfort.

COMMENTARY: All of Mari's verbal aggressiveness is on display here. Her language just splutters forth at great speed; she speaks before she thinks. A romantic encounter is treated first as a boxing match, then as a dance, finally as a road race with hairpin turns. The speech is full of physical possibilities. Marie speaks in a tough, Northern working-class accent which is full of colourful and explosive verbs and nouns. She's hot-tempered and adventurous. What she most hates is being stuck at home with a daughter who barely speaks. The fiery teenager in her has never cooled down.

Serious Money
Caryl Churchill

Act 2. The first class cabin of an airplane. The late 1980s.

Jacinta Condor (20s-30s) is a highly successful and ruthless Peruvian businesswoman. She is a wheeler dealer who trades in people. This is the era of the 'Big Bang' in London's financial centre and megascale greed for serious money. She is flying into London First Class, where she will stay in great style at the Savoy Hotel, to do some deals. She is 'A very smart lady from South America who comes here every winter./ Europe sends aid, her family says thanks/And buys Eurobonds in Swiss banks.' In this speech she reveals some of her business philosophy.

JACINTA. Flight to England that little grey island in the clouds where governments don't fall overnight and children don't sell themselves in the street and my money is safe. I'll buy a raincoat, I'll meet Jake Todd, I'll stay at the Savoy by the stream they call a river with its Bloody Tower and dead queens, a river is too wide to bridge. The unfinished bridge across the canyon where the road ends in the air, waiting for dollars. The office blocks father started, imagining glass, leather, green screens, the city rising high into the sky, but the towers stopped short, cement, wires, the city spreading wider instead with a blur of shacks, miners coming down from the mountains as the mines close. The International Tin Council, what a scandal, thank God I wasn't in tin, the price of copper ruined by the frozen exchange rate, the two rates, and the government will not let us mining companies exchange enough dollars at the better rate, they insist we help the country in this crisis, I do not want to help, I want to be rich, I close my mines and sell my copper on the London Metal Exchange. It is all because of the debt that will never be paid

88

because we have to borrow more and more to pay the interest on the money that came from oil when OPEC had too much money and your western banks wanted to lend it to us because who else would pay such high interest, needing it so badly? Father got his hands on enough of it but what happened, massive inflation, lucky he'd put the money somewhere safe, the Swiss mountains so white from the air like our mountains but the people rich with cattle and clocks and secrets, the American plains yellow with wheat, the green English fields where lords still live in grey stone, all with such safe banks and good bonds and exciting gambles, so as soon as any dollars or pounds come, don't let them go into our mines or our coffee or look for a sea of oil under the jungle, no get it out quickly to the western banks (a little money in cocaine, that's different). Peru leads the way resisting the IMF, refusing to pay the interest, but I don't want to make things difficult for the banks, I prefer to support them, why should my money stay in Peru and suffer? The official closing price yesterday for grade A copper was 878-8.5, three months 900.5-1, final kerb close 901-2. Why bother to send aid so many miles, put it straight into my eurobonds.

COMMENTARY: If Jacinta's speech sounds like a huge muddle, it is. Her view of London is colored by her Latin American vision. What she describes is an international financial market which has finally reached into and is pillaging the Third World. The speech is full of the kind of landmarks that denote wealth: grand hotels, monuments and bridges, houses, office buildings, mines and banks. In fact, the whole world is viewed from on high like some huge global Monopoly board. Pieces and money are moved about in a frenzy of ongoing trading. There is nothing personal or human in Jacinta's speech. You keep your eyes on the shifting prices and nothing else. But notice too what sensual pleasure she takes in what she says.

Shades
Sharman Macdonald

Act 2. The Powder Room of a posh hotel. Glasgow in the 1950s.

Pearl (late 30s) is a widow with a ten-year-old son. She has a good job as the suit buyer for a department store. But the thought of becoming middle-aged depresses and frightens her. Although she is haunted by the memory of her dead husband and by the powerful love she still feels for him she wants to live life to the full. She dreams not only of finding romance again but she also wants her son to have a father. She has been going out with Callum for some time but she is undecided as to whether or not she is in love with him. She is preparing for a special night out with him: 'I'm going to dance. I'm going to laugh a bit. Maybe I'll have a drink. Maybe I'll smoke a cigarette after the toast to the Queen. I'll eat and I'll talk.' In this scene, which opens the second act, Pearl is alone in the powder room. It is late in the evening and the dinner dance has come to an end. She has washed her hands and is staring at her reflection in the mirror.

PEARL. Look at that face. That's a terrible face. Fancy waking up every morning to a face like that. What man would want to? Good God, I don't want to. What's that look in its eye? I know what you want. I know. You're cheap, that's what you are. Aye, and you're common too. Do you hear me? Behave yourself. Go home before you do yourself a damage. You've drunk too much. And he's drunk too much. Go home before it ends in tears. (*She gets close to her reflection in the mirror.*) You're not listening to me. Don't you come to me with that face. That's a night face. That face. A 'come to bed' face. You're not going out there with a face like that, and you needn't think it. I'll fix you. (*She wipes at her mouth to get the lipstick off. Looks back at the mirror.*) My God you're

90

bold. Look at those eyes. What are you up to, eh? Sneaky. What are you going to do, eh? Oh my God. You'll do it without me. Murky eyes. I don't trust them. They'll ask for what they want, those eyes. No bother. I'll fix that face, and you'll not stop me. Anything could happen to a woman that wears a face like that. And none of it nice. It's an open invitation, that face. (*She touches the reflection.*) Don't be too obvious. Never put all your cards on the table at once. Do you hear me? Are you listening to me? No man wants a thing if he thinks it's offered to him on a plate. (*Snatches her hand away.*) Take off that face and put a good one on. That's a wicked face. That's the face of a trollop if ever I saw one. (*She washes her face at the sink. Looks for a towel.*) Damn. (*Dries it on the hem of her dress. Looks back at the mirror.*) All gone. Pity, eh? That's your old mum's face. Your goody, goody face. Your 'I know what's good for you' face. Your 'I'm telling you' face. A mother's face. That wee bit tired. Strain round the eyes. A bit wan. That's the face that turns your hair white. Nothing'll happen to that face. (*She turns away from the mirror. Looks at her watch. Peers at it.*) You're useless you. Must be late. I'm that tired. I'm that weary. Home to bed, that's the thing. Straight home. Straight to bed. Leave the night here. Don't ask for the moon. (*She peeps back over her shoulder.*) Who are you kidding? You'll not fool me, and you needn't think it. You're not tired. Not tired at all. You're raring to go, you. (*Takes a decision. Slashes lipstick at her mouth.*) We'll go halfway. We've some fun left in us yet, and why not? Our life's not over. We've the world in front of us. A halfway face. It can take its chance. A 'maybe maybe' face. A bit of lipstick. There's no harm. Nun's eyes and a harlot's mouth. We'll leave it to him. Choice. What do you say, face? He can take his choice. We'll not tell him what we want. Keep him guessing. Eh, face? (*Touches her harlot's lips.*)

COMMENTARY: The mirror image provides you with an excellent focus. In fact, Pearl is constantly shifting her focus nearer to and further from the reflection in the mirror. The monologue is full of attraction *and* repulsion. Two parts of Pearl are on display: her 'Nun's eyes and a harlot's mouth.' The normal act of making-up becomes a self-interrogation. Pearl is also tipsy. So her tongue's been loosened by drink. She's also tired. But she's doing-up her face so that she can go back and perform again for a man. A lot of her concentration is on her eyes. She sounds like a mother talking to a wayward daughter.

The Sisters Rosensweig
Wendy Wasserstein

Act 2, scene 2. A sitting room in Queen Anne's Gate, London. A weekend in late August 1991.

Gorgeous Teitelbaum (46) is married to an attorney and has four kids. She has blossomed from a suburban Massachusetts housewife into a popular phone-in radio agony aunt, 'Dr Gorgeous'. (She has no formal qualifications, the 'Dr' is merely for show.) As a confirmed chatterbox, she has found the perfect outlet for her gregarious and vivacious 'people' skills. 'Funsy' is her favourite catch phrase, and she wants the world to be a 'funsy' place. She is in London leading a tour group of twenty ladies from the Temple Beth El in Newton, Massachusetts, and she is also in town to celebrate her sister Sara's birthday. She is a 'very pretty but overdone woman . . . She wears a fake Chanel suit with too many accessories.' She loves shopping and aspires to own genuine designer garments. In this scene she enters, drenched, with an umbrella and a shopping bag. She launches into this speech detailing her disastrous day for the benefit of her two sisters.

GORGEOUS. [I'd rather stand.] Rabbi Pearlstein says I should finish the tour and come home.
[PFENI. You called him?]
Let me tell you that, thanks to both of you, this has not been an especially enjoyable trip for me. I've spent two days schlepping around London with the sisterhood and two nights having my own sisters tell me everything I do is wrong. Then I decide to treat myself to a little something because I can't bear the stress anymore.
[SARA. Georgeous, I'm –
GORGEOUS. Let me finish.] So I go to eight shoe stores on Sloane Street – one nicer than the other. I spread my toes in

93

Tanino Crisci, I slide into the Ferragamos with the bows, and I even clip-clop in royal velvet Manulo Blanchiki frontless, backless mules. And finally, I make my choice – an exquisite pair I know I've seen before on the feet of Fergie or Di or Lady Michael of Kent. They're the softest grosgrain, on the shapeliest heel I've ever seen. I take out my charge card – with tax it comes to two hundred pounds – that's four hundred dollars for a pair of shoes – don't tell me that's insane, I know, but I'm tired and I decide for once I'm worth it.

[SARA. Of course!

GORGEOUS. I'm not finished!] So I'm walking past Harrods in my new shoes, and for the first time since I arrived here I feel like a person. I debate taking the taxi back to Queen Anne's Gate, and I decide that just because I have shoes like Princess Di, I shouldn't spend like her. So I go into the tube stop at Kensington Station. I get on the escalator, and guess what happens – the shapely goddamned heel gets caught and rips the hell out of my four-hundred-dollar shoe! And all along a blind man with a cup is watching me. And I think to myself, I'm being punished by God because I did not give that man money, even if he is a fake!

COMMENTARY: The comic effect of this speech is bitterly blunted by the fact that Gorgeous has been exposed as a fraud. She is not Princess Di but just another American tourist who's run-up a big bill with her credit card. Everything from her name to her profession to her clothes are all fake. Getting her heel caught and broken is like having the bubble burst. Even a blind man can see that, she seems to be saying. But while she was purchasing those shoes she felt, for the first time since arriving in London, like a real person.

Six Degrees of Separation
John Guare

One Act. A smart New York apartment on Fifth Avenue.

Ouisa (short for Louisa) Kittredge (43) is 'very attractive'. She and her husband Flanders are successful art dealers. They have three children who are all students. She is an accomplished and witty hostess; the mistress of the one-line put-down. The calm of their affluent, sheltered lives is threatened when Paul, a young black man, arrives out of the blue on their doorstep. He is offered refuge in their home when it becomes apparent that he has been mugged in Central Park, is a university friend of their children and is also the son of the famous black actor Sidney Poitier. The truth however is that Paul is a conman and fantasist who has duped the Kittredges as he has previously deceived several other victims of his scam. Paul regales his hosts with tales of his famous 'father', which they eagerly lap up, and he even offers them parts in 'father's' latest production: the movie version of the hit musical Cats. *In another subsequent con, Paul, pretending that his 'father' is now Flan, successfully dupes a young aspiring actor out of a thousand dollars. When the actor commits suicide the police eventually catch up with Paul and he is hauled off to jail. In this scene Ouisa and Flan are trying to come to terms with just how this all happened and what they really feel about Paul. Ouisa is forced to question the values of the gossipy, materialistic world she inhabits.*

OUISA. He wanted to be us. Everything we are in the world, this paltry thing – our life – he wanted it. He stabbed himself to get in here. He envied us. We're not enough to be envied.
[FLAN. Like the papers said. We have hearts.]
Having a heart is not the point. We were hardly taken in. We believed him – for a few hours. He did more for us in a few hours than our children ever did. He wanted to be your

95

child. Don't let that go. He sat out in that park and said that man is my father. He's in trouble and we don't know how to help him.

[FLAN. Help him? He could've killed me. And you.]

You were attracted to him –

[FLAN. Cut me out of that pathology! You are on your own –]

Attracted by youth and his talent and the embarrassing prospect of being in the movie version of *Cats*. Did you put that in your *Times* piece? And we turn him into an anecdote to dine out on. Or dine in on. But it was an experience. I will not turn him into an anecdote. How do we fit what happened to us into life without turning it into an anecdote with no teeth and a punch line you'll mouth over and over for years to come. 'Tell the story about the imposter who came into our lives – ' 'That reminds me of the time this boy – .' And we become these human juke boxes spilling out these anecdotes. But it was an experience. How do we *keep* the experience?

COMMENTARY: Ouisa has clearly had an 'experience'. But she only goes far enough to say that and no further towards understanding what it all means. She searches for significance in the event. She's also trying to locate her identity through the event. Ouisa is a seeker after change. She's looking for someone – anyone – who will come into her comfortable, upper-middle-class existence and rearrange all the pieces. Paul the conman does just that. But rather than feel anger and resentment, Ouisa feels only acceptance and even thanks. Her life, after all, is a kind of fraud as well. She's an impostor herself. And maybe that is why she identifies with Paul so fully.

Some Americans Abroad
Richard Nelson

Act 1, scene 4. The bar of the Lyttleton Theatre, in the Royal National Theatre, London.

Joanne Smith (26) is an American who has been living in London for sixteen months and is married to an Englishman, James, who is a successful businessman in the City. She likes London but has come to resent American tourists: 'I used to feel a little funny about it. They are after all from my country. But – (Beat.) Then you hear them shout . . . Sometimes when I'm in a shop I try not to say anything. I just point. Maybe they think I'm English or something. Maybe that I don't even speak English. That I'm foreign. So I point.' She is a graduate of a New England liberal arts college and she helps to arrange theatre visits to London for tour groups from the college. Her husband works long hours and she hints at being bored and lonely. She wants to fit in but has not yet found her niche. In this scene she is chatting with some of the faculty about one of the plays she has booked for them.

[JOE. Joanne's been to the play we're seeing this afternoon. She loved it.

JOANNE. It's very funny.] I love those old Aldwych farces. They're so English.

[JOE. They really are.]

I don't think they'd work at all in America today, do you?

[JOE. I can't see how. It takes a special . . .

I know what you mean.] (*Beat.*) James's family is right out of one of those plays actually. (*Laughs to herself.*) The first time I met them – . They don't live posh or anything like that, but there is a cook. She used to be James's nanny. (*Beat.*) One of the family, she is. And everyone is always saying that. Helen from Glasgow. (*Beat.*) They could not have been

97

kinder to me. James's father, Freddy – he insists I call him Freddy – and once he gets into a chair you begin to wonder if he'll ever move out of it. (*Beat.*) Or so his mother says. James's sister made us all watch the telly. James tried to argue but I said I'd love to. I'd only been here a month and I'd hardly got used to English telly so I thought here was my chance to ask questions. (*Beat.*) So this man comes on; he tries to make some jokes which are not funny, I think to myself. Then he says something like: 'The girl went up to the boy and put her hand into his – .' He pauses and a middle-aged woman completes the sentence with: ' – her hand into his *golf bag*!' And everyone laughs. (*Beat.*) Even James laughed I noticed. This is peculiar I think to myself. (*Beat.*) 'Into his golf bag.' She continues now ' – and pulls out a club which she used to wiggle his – .' She pauses and a middle-aged man now completes the sentence with: 'Wiggle his *tee* out of the ground.' (*Short pause. She sips her tea.*) [JOE. Huh.]

This goes on and on. And when it ends the man who started it all drops his trousers to reveal that his underpants look like the British flag. (*Short pause.*) What's amazing about England is that in time you begin to find this sort of thing funny as well. (*Beat.*) Or so I'm told. James says it's the weather. (*Beat.*) In any event, I don't think a good old Aldwych farce would work in America.

attached to each encounter. To her eyes and ears Americans and Britons truly seem to be two people divided by a common tongue; two cultures that will never sit easily together.

Talking Heads
Alan Bennett

Her Last Chance. Lesley's flat. Afternoon.

Lesley (early 30s) is an aspiring actress. She has had a succession of walk-on parts in TV and film but her career has never quite taken off. 'People who know me tell me I'm a very serious person, only it's funny, I never get to do serious parts. The parts I get offered tend to be fun-loving girls who take life as it comes and aren't afraid of a good time should the opportunity arise-type-thing.' Lesley takes her career very seriously and is prepared to do almost anything. 'I am professional to my fingertips.' Even in the smallest of parts she analyses her character scrupulously to find motivation. She is gregarious and assertive but her pedantic and obstinate manner can often be quite grating for those around her. 'Now my hobby is people. I collect people.' In this section, taken from a longer extended monologue, Lesley describes her audition for a film.

LESLEY. I know something about personality. There's a chapter about it in this book I'm reading. It's by an American. They're the experts where personality is concerned, the Americans; they've got it down to a fine art. It makes a big thing of interviews so I was able to test it out.

The director's not very old, blue suit, tie loose, sleeves turned back. I put him down as a university type. Said his name was Simon, which I instantly committed to memory. (That's one of the points in the book: purpose and use of name.) He said, 'Forgive this crazy time.' I said, 'I'm sorry, Simon?' He said, 'Like 9.30 in the morning.' I said, 'Simon. The day begins when the day begins. You're the director.' He said, 'Yes, well. Can you tell me what you've done?'

I said, 'Where you may have seen me, Simon, is in *Tess.*

Roman Polanski. I played Chloë.' 'I don't remember her,' he said. 'Is she in the book?' I said, 'Book? This is *Tess*, Simon. Roman Polanski. Chloë was the one on the back of the farm cart wearing a shawl. The shawl was original nineteenth-century embroidery. All hand done. Do you know Roman, Simon?' He said, 'Not personally, no.' I said, 'Physically he's quite small but we had a very good working relationship. Very open.' He said that was good, because Travis in the film was very open. I said, 'Travis? That's an interesting name, Simon.' He said, 'Yes. She's an interesting character, she spends most of the film on the deck of a yacht.' I said, 'Yacht? That's interesting, Simon. My brother-in-law has a small power boat berthed at Ipswich.' He said, 'Well! Snap!' I said, 'Yes, small world!' He said, 'In an ideal world, Lesley, I'd be happy to sit here chatting all day but I have a pretty tight schedule and, although I know it's only 9.30 in the morning, could I see you in your bra and panties?' I said, '9.30 in the morning, 10.30 at night, we're both professionals, Simon, but', I said, 'could we just put another bar on because if we don't you won't be able to tell my tits from goose-pimples.' He had to smile. That was another of the sections in the personality book: humour, usefulness of in breaking the ice.

When I'd got my things off he said, 'Well, you've passed the physical. Now the oral. Do you play chess?' I said, 'Chess, Simon? Do you mean the musical?' He said, 'No, the game.' I said, 'As a matter of fact, Simon, I don't. Is that a problem?' He said, 'Not if you water-ski. Travis is fundamentally an outdoor girl, but we thought it might be fun to make her an intellectual on the side.' I said, 'Well Simon, I'm very happy to learn both chess and water-skiing, but could I make a suggestion? Reading generally indicates a studious temperament and I'm a very convincing reader,' I said, 'because it's something I frequently do in real life.' I could tell he was impressed. And so I said, 'Another suggestion I could make would be to kit Travis out with some glasses. Spectacles, Simon. These days they're not unbecoming and if you put Travis in spectacles with something in paperback, that says it all.' He said, 'You've been most helpful.' I said, 'The paperback could be something about the environment or, if you want to maintain the water-skiing theme, something about water-skiing and the environment possibly. I mean, Lake Windermere.'

He was showing me out by this time but I said, 'One last thought, Simon, and that is a briefcase. Put Travis in a bikini and give her a briefcase and you get the best of every possible world.' He said, 'I'm most grateful. You've given me a lot of ideas.' I said, 'Goodbye, Simon. I hope we can work together.' The drill for saying goodbye is you take the person's hand and then put your other hand over theirs, clasp it warmly while at the same time looking into their eyes, smiling and reiterating their name. This lodges you in their mind apparently. So I did all that, only going downstairs I had another thought and I popped back. He was on the phone. 'You won't believe this,' he was saying. I said, 'Don't hang up, Simon, only I just wanted to make it crystal clear that when I said briefcase I didn't mean the old-fashioned type ones, there are new briefcases now that open up and turn into a mini writing-desk. Being an up-to-the-minute girl, that would probably be the kind of briefcase Travis would have. She could be sitting in a wet bikini with a briefcase open on her knee. I've never seen that on screen so it would be some kind of first. Ciao, Simon. Take care.' (*Pause*.) That was last Friday. The book's got charts where you check your interview score. Mine was 75. Very good to excellent. Actually, I'm surprised they haven't telephoned.

COMMENTARY: Lesley is a great believer in self-improvement. It's one of the tools she uses to try and get ahead (or understand why she *doesn't* get ahead). She's also a terrible snob and tries to match wits with Simon the director. The speech builds by the process of accumulation: each detail she adds only undermines her chance at the role. The monologue is also an excellent guide as to what *not* to do during an audition. Lesley is far too chatty and familiar; she steps over the boundary. She offers endless hints which seem only to be at odds with the director's thoughts. The actor must be careful not to overplay the comedy here but to let the words and thoughts guide you. In the end you have to decide how much of what Lesley says is pure bluff to hide rejection or just dumb confidence.

Talking in Tongues
Winsome Pinnock

Act 1, scene 5. A room in a London house. A New Year's Eve party.

Irma (30) is black, bald and androgynous. There is something both enigmatic and charismatic about her. She is articulate and talkative, especially when she is the subject. As she says, 'I myself have never had a problem with people looking at me. It's being ignored I can't stand.' She sits cross-legged and wears a multicoloured jump suit and trainers. She exudes a centred and confident quality. She has arrived typically late at the party which is already well under way. In this scene she is alone with Leela and she launches into this speech soon after they introduce themselves. This is her only appearance in the play.

IRMA. You don't say much, do you? Not that it matters. I can talk the hind legs off an armchair. (*Pause.*) I was born in south London thirty years ago. My birth was the occasion of great trauma for my mother who, prior to going into labour, had witnessed the strange couplings of common or garden slugs on her kitchen floor at midnight. It wasn't the bizarreness of their copulation that struck her but the realisation that each partner had both projectile and receptacle – she was very fastidious – which, in effect, made the sex act redundant as a particularly flexible slug could impregnate itself. That such a phenomenon existed on God's earth – she was also very superstitious – underminded the very tenets by which she'd thus far kept her life together. She felt cheated. If God had seen fit to bestow this gift upon human beings then she would not have had to undergo the ritual Friday Night Fuck, a particularly vigorous, not to mention careless, session of which had resulted in my conception. She was overwhelmed by the depth of her anger, and the shock of it propelled her into labour. The doctors didn't know how to tell her at first. It doesn't happen very often, but sometimes a child is born with both receptacle and projectile nestling between its legs. I was such a child and the doctors told my mother that she had to make a choice, or I would be plagued by severe mental confusion and distress for the rest of my life. Of course she didn't know which way to turn. In the end she settled on getting rid of the male appendage, not least because she held the things in contempt but also because she felt that black men were too often in the limelight, and that a woman might quietly get things done while those who undermined her were looking the other way. However, she hadn't reckoned with the fact that she had already become attached to me and found me perfect the way I was. So even while the surgeon was sharpening his knives my mother had wrapped me in an old shawl, woven by her own grandmother, and taken me home. I hope I'm not boring you.

COMMENTARY: Irma is totally self-possessed. She gives us her entire birth history and it sounds like a curious sort of biology lesson. Why she tells us all this is never entirely clear. But it's a vivid tale and Irma must come across as a compelling storyteller with a language all her own. She's very confident and, unlike the other women in the play, Irma feels at peace with herself and confident of her unusual sexuality. She can literally go in any direction like the slugs she describes. Her function in the play is to contradict the stultifying middle-class values that inhibit the romantic lives of the other female characters.

Ten Tiny Fingers, Nine Tiny Toes
Sue Townsend

Scene 8. A two-bedded room in the Buxton Maternity Unit, Derbyshire. The year 2001.

Lucinda Darling (30s) has been married 'forever' to Ralph Darling who is the boss of a drinking straw factory in Derbyshire. They are a conventional, well-to-do couple. As inveterate snobs, their main concern is keeping up appearances. The only thing lacking in their tidy lives is a baby; they have not been able to conceive successfully due to Ralph's low sperm count: 'We examined our marriage for obvious and hidden defects. But we concluded that in spite of certain difficulties, we'd make fantastic parents.' To remedy this situation they decide to buy a baby. In the year 2001 this is accepted practice, not only can you buy babies (if, that is, you come from the correct social class) but you can select their exact genetic make-up. Lucinda opts to give birth herself rather than have a laboratory reared baby. They are guaranteed 'a perfect baby: blonde, blue eyes, 5 foot 6 inches at maturity'. Lucinda is 'glamorous in her pregnancy, lace negligée, fluffy mules, full make-up'. In this scene Lucinda has just been informed by her consultant that the baby she is expecting has a defect – she only has nine toes. As a result 'when she is born she will be taken away immediately, and she will die in her sleep'. In this speech Lucinda reacts to this news.

LUCINDA. Could I please keep the baby sir? I'm willing to drop a grade. I could live a Grade Four life. Leeds and its environs is quite a pleasant place.

[CRUDWELL. The latest regulations apply to all grades. Of course Grade Fives are not allowed to breed at all. (*He looks at* DOT, *she stares back at him. She would like to shout and scream, but daren't.*)

DOT. You won't take mine off me.

CRUDWELL (*brightly*). We have made other arrangements

106

for your child. A boy, a perfectly healthy boy. Ten tiny fingers, ten tiny toes. Everything in its place. Quite an exceptional child. We are very interested in him.

DOT. His name is Peter.

CRUDWELL. Is it? I'll remember that. Peter Bird.]

[No,] I'm afraid you don't understand, I don't mind about the toe. What's a missing toe? She'll have nine others to compensate for the lack of one. I must keep her, I've carried her around for nine months and I've grown rather fond of her, in fact very fond. And we've paid a great deal of money for this baby. We've liquidised a share portfolio to pay for her nursery. The decorator's bill alone! Blush pink walls, white ceiling and a lilac dado. We've bought the furniture: a wicker basket lined in handmade lace. A patchwork quilt which took six women five months to complete. A changing mat on a table of a suitable height to prevent back injury. An Edwardian nursing chair. Her clothes are waiting for her! They're in an old sea captain's chest. My husband has ordered six cases of genuine Australian champagne from an ex-directory wholesaler, Freephone 001122. I've enrolled for a part-time degree in child nutrition – she won't be allowed to eat sugar or salt. I will train her palette – I was 25 before I enjoyed a quail's egg.

[CRUDWELL. Now stop it.]

She's going to the best playgroup in Greater Manchester. Ralph knows influential people. I've ordered a sand-pit. I've chosen her name. Her pram cover is hand embroidered, copied from the one Zanna's mother gave her for Phoenix in *Flippers Retreat*. The women stitching it went blind – that's how small the stitches are. I've chosen her friends! I've *pored* over genealogical text books. I know who she's going to marry! His name is Crispin Browne-Hogg and he's two and a half years old and he's going to be a plastic surgeon. We've planned a huge party for next Saturday – my deep freeze is packed to the gills with frozen canapes – look! Look! Frostbite! So you see, don't you, Mr Crudwell, that you cannot take my daughter away and kill her, because of all the aforementioned arrangements?

COMMENTARY: In among all the expansive comic touches the actor must isolate a woman's profound terror at having her baby taken away. The comic and the tragic must mix in equal proportion. All the talk is a stalling mechanism to avoid the worst. Like all absurdist comedy, the darkness of a situation is suddenly filled with radiant light through the cataloguing of exaggerated details like 'A patchwork quilt which took six women five months to complete.' Everything that's been bought for the new baby's comfort sounds like a series of product advertisements. Yet this is a world where commercial expedients rule over human needs. Children and their surroundings must be perfect in every way.

Three Birds Alighting on a Field
Timberlake Wertenbaker

Act 1, scene 1. To the audience.

Biddy Andreas (30s) is married to Giorgos, 'Yoyo', a wealthy Greek tycoon. Biddy is presented as the product of a cloistered upper-class upbringing. She is honest, unaffected, but a bit dim. She has children from an earlier marriage which ended in divorce. Her husband is socially ambitious and he hopes that the well-bred and well-connected Biddy will facilitate his entry into English high society. He is prepared to do anything to gain social acceptance and become an English gentleman. Biddy leads an extremely comfortable, uncomplicated life, 'I have nothing to be angry about. I'm married. I'm rich. I have a lovely big garden.' In this speech Biddy reflects on how her life changed when she married Yoyo.

BIDDY. I didn't at first understand what was happening. For someone like me, who was used to being tolerated, it came as a surprise. You see, before, everything I said was passed over. Well, smiled at, but the conversation would continue elsewhere. I was like the final touches of a well decorated house. It gives pleasure, but you don't notice it. England still had women who went to good schools, and looked after large homes in the country, horses, dogs, children, that sort of thing, that was my voice. Tony – that's my first husband – said he found my conversation comforting background noise when he read the papers. But then, silences began to greet everything I said. Heavy silences. I thought there was something wrong. Then I noticed they were waiting for more words, and these words had suddenly taken on a tremendous importance. But I was still saying the same things. You know, about shopping at Harrods, and trains being slow, and good avocados being hard to come by, and cleaning ladies even harder. And then, I understood. You see, I had become tremendously rich. Not myself, but my husband, my second husband. And when you're that rich, nothing you do is trivial. If I took an hour telling a group of people how I had looked for and not found a good pair of gardening gloves, if I went into every detail of the weeks I had spent on this search, the phone bills I had run up, the catalogues I had returned, they were absolutely riveted. Riveted. Because it seemed everything I did, now that I was so tremendously wealthy because of my second husband, mattered. Mattered tremendously. I hadn't expected this, because you see, my husband was foreign, Greek actually, and I found that not – well, not quite properly English you know, to be married to a Greek – after all, Biddy *Andreas*? I could imagine my headmistress – we had a Greek girl at Benenden, we all turned down invitations to her island – and Yoyo – that's my husband, George, Giorgos, actually – he didn't even go to school here – but he was so rich and I became used to it – him, and me: being important.

COMMENTARY: Biddy has not been a person but an accessory in a *Town & Country* lifestyle: 'I was like the final touches of a well decorated house'; a good wife to a husband of means. She speaks in the strangulated fashion of someone who has not had the chance to form a complete identity but has always been subservient. There is no anger in her voice, only calmness and control. She is full of poise and breeding. Nothing she says sounds vulgar. When she becomes rich, however, her life as a cipher suddenly takes on new value. Significantly, people pay her attention. And this is when things get complicated for her. Suddenly she is a means for others to get to her husband's money; a valuable and important conduit. Yet she does have an ironic sense of herself and her worth. And this must come across as an attractive side in performance. She's probably not as vapid as she seems.

Three Hotels
Jon Robin Baitz

Part Two: Be Careful. A beach front cabana. St. Thomas, Virgin Islands.

Barbara Hoyle (40s) is married to Kenneth Hoyle, a rising vice-president with an American multinational corporation which sells baby-milk formula to undeveloped countries. His job has required them to be posted throughout the Third World. During their stay in Brazil their sixteen-year-old son, Brandon, was casually killed on the beach for his watch. This tragic event finally forced Barbara to confront the deaths of the thousands of faceless babies murdered by the products sold by the company that employs her husband. She becomes increasingly critical and alienated from her husband. Their once passionate marriage is now arid and soulless. As the personal and the political become indistinguishable in Barbara's mind she suffers a crisis of conscience. In this scene she is recalling a frank and controversial confessional speech that she delivered that morning to the wives of company men about to be posted overseas for the first time.

BARBARA. I say this to them, and I mean it, I want to help. 'Be careful of spending too much time alone. Learn the language – whatever you do – learn the language fast. The silence in those houses they find for you with the servants – it can overwhelm you.' I smile. A sister. 'Look. I'm gonna level with you,' – now I know I'm hitting my stride, doing a sort of a midwife routine – 'they say it's an adventure and it is. But it's also a sacrifice. You're giving up things here and when you come back, it'll never be the same – make sure your husband understands this. Make sure he knows that what you're coming back to is not the . . .' (*Pause.*) 'Of course, not all of you will come back with a dead son.' (*Beat.* BARBARA *smiles*

III

sadly.) Have I crossed a line? I never talk about this. But it seems false – mealy-mouthed not to make mention of it – and I – to tell you the truth – I am beginning to realize it is expected of me. I go on. 'Most likely, percentage-wise very few of you will come back without a child – but if you do . . . come back . . . with a coffin . . .' (*Beat*.) 'Talk about it.' They nod. They *know*. They're women for God's sake, not just DARs. I shake my head. 'You know – we hear the news, "We're moving overseas." Maybe we're sitting in the kitchen alone after they've gone to the office, having that quiet cup of afternoon coffee and the phone rings and it's your husband and he says, "I was right. We're going to . . . Surinam or Sri Lanka or *Rio*." And there is this sense of . . . "oh it's a mission" . . . that sort of overtakes you. A dream. Remember, it is not . . . your mission. Your husband's mission is not – your mission. Be careful . . . that you keep the clarity of your own life.' I pause. They are nodding. 'Or you will come back and you will have . . . dust. You will have nothing.' Silence.

COMMENTARY: The speech alternates between control and loss of control as Barbara's own personal tragedy stands between her and her audience. She worries that the mere mention of the young man's death means she will have stepped over the line of propriety. Suddenly, after the first pause, it is just blurted out. Strangely, though, the speech is never too explicit or clear. Macabre elements emerge (like the mention of a 'coffin'), but Barbara speaks mainly in codes to couch her grief and she shrouds unpleasant details behind pauses. She also disguises her alienation from her husband ('Your husband's mission is not – your mission'). The speech is meant to sound like a corporate or military training exercise yet it keeps breaking down and stalling.

To
Jim Cartwright

One Act. A pub in the North of England.

Mrs Iger (50s) has come to the pub with her husband, Mr Iger, who she dominates. They appear to be a very ordinary married couple. But she is very scathing of her 'Mr Feeble' and his endless 'cock-ups'. She even makes him sleep in a separate bed. In this speech, with her arms folded and perched on a bar stool, she reveals her notion of an ideal man.

MRS IGER. I love big men. Big quiet strong men. That's all I want. I love to tend to them. I like to have grace and flurry round them. I like their temple arms and pillar legs and synagogue chests and big mouth and teeth and tongue like an elephant's ear. And big carved faces like a naturreal cliff side, and the Roman empire bone work. And you can really dig deep into 'em, can't you? And there's so much. Gargantuan man, like a Roman Empire, with a voice he hardly uses, but when he does it's all rumbling under his breast plate. So big, big hands, big everything. Like sleeping by a mountain side. Carved men. It's a thrill if you see them run, say for a bus, pounding up the pavement. Good big man, thick blood through tubular veins, squirting and washing him out. It must be like a bloody big red cavernous car wash in there, in him, and all his organs and bits hanging from the rib roof, getting a good daily drenching in this good red blood. They are so bloody big you think they'll never die, and that's another reason you want them. Bloody ox men, Hercules, Thor, Chuck Connors, come on, bring your heads down and take from my 'ickle hand. Let me groom and coddle you. And herd you. Yes, let me gather all you big men of our Isles and

113

herd you up and lead you across America. You myth men. Myth men. Myth men. Big men love ya.

COMMENTARY: The men of Mrs Iger's dreams are rock-solid and godly. Though not quite stretching back as far as Neolithic men, she does like men with the strength of a Roman legion. She talks like an archeologist unearthing a lost species or a biologist charting the circulation inside a giant. She also speaks like an Old Testament prophetess reaching back through time to find exactly the right means of expressing her desires. There is nothing contemporary about Mrs Iger's desires. Great movie stars and lithe young sensual men do not figure in her pantheon. She loves myth men.

Woman (30s-40s) speaks of the pain of being the 'other' woman. She is slightly drunk. She arrives just as last orders are being called in the pub.

WOMAN (*to audience*). Are they still serving? I mustn't leave this corner for the moment. I'm the 'Other Woman', come where she shouldn't to look at my man. My man and his wife. I've not come incognito either. I've come as my bloody self, drinky, smart, a little crumpled, used to being dressed up at the wrong time in the wrong places. In the only car on a car park after dark. In strange houses in the afternoon. At bus stops in last night's make-up. And I'm not having it no, no more Mister. (*She takes out a fag, fumbles with it, drops it.*) I've come here tonight, so he can see us both. Not one in one world and one in another, but both under the same light and choose. (*As in a child's choosing rhyme.*) Ip, dip, ip, dip, ip, dip. You see this is the last time I'm going to love. I haven't got it in me to go again. So it's to be him, or it's to be something else, but not another man. No, no more. Where's that fagarette? Did I drop it? Toots to it, toots to the lot of it. Did he look then? (*She tugs at her scarf, it falls.*) He did, I'm sure. Oh Jesu! Jesu! I

114

want him. I want to wave and scream. She doesn't know, you know. I can tell, see, see that laugh she makes, too free, too free by far. I think. That's how it is in flick and shadow land, it's all thinking of others and their movements and I am sick to the soul with it. What will he do? What will she say? Will he come? Will he cancel? Is that the door? Was that the car? Dare I shower? Will he ring? Most times these wives, you know, they don't even want them. They won't have love with them, you know. They put them down, you know. But they won't let them loose. My God, they will not let them loosey. And I love loosey. Oh my God, he's coming over. Face him, face him. No shift, shift, shift. Face him. Shift. (*She turns away.*)

COMMENTARY: The Woman drinks to bolster her confidence. As the alcohol loosens her tongue, her speech becomes increasingly confessional. She must have been building up her courage all evening since she's only just made it in time for last orders. She is in a nervous, fumbling panic, ducking, bobbing and dropping things. But notice that despite all of this she keeps her 'man' always in her line of vision. She is full of anger and frustration with her uncertain and tentative life which is led strictly in the shadows. It is interesting that the playwright does not give her a name and this accentuates her anonymity. She is at the end of her tether. She wants to be acknowledged, embraced and loved out in the open for everyone to see. Part of the speech is like a pep talk as she tries to build up the confidence to confront her 'man' face to face. She is like an actor preparing to go on stage. But she loses her nerve at the last moment. You must establish the convention that the audience is in a busy pub full of noise, distractions and, most important of all, 'my man'.

The Woman Destroyed
Simone de Beauvoir (adapted by Diana Quick)

Section III: I've Got to Get Back to a Normal Life. The drawing room of Murielle's flat. New Year's Eve 1967.

Murielle (43) is separated from her husband Tristan, who has custody of their eleven-year-old son Francis. In return for her son Tristan has given her 'an allowance and the flat'. She was raised with the expectation that love, marriage and babies were to be her destiny, and now she finds herself bereft of all three. She has been married once before to Albert, and Sylvie, her daughter from that marriage, committed suicide when she was seventeen. Murielle blames herself for this tragedy. She reflects on what might have been, of what would have happened if she had gone off with Florent, a serious admirer from her youth. She has no resources, no skills, no ambition and no confidence to help her escape her predicament. She has become imprisoned by her own limitations and her only recourse is rage. As she says, 'I sit here stewing in my own juice I'm fed up with it, fed up with it . . . I'm bored stiff with being bored.' She is alone on New Year's Eve and is reflecting on her life.

MURIELLE. Shit I'm gasping for a drink I'm starving but it would kill me to get out of my chair and go to the kitchen.

You freeze in this dump and then when I turn the heating up the air dries out, my mouth is all dry and my nose is burning. What a cock-up. They know how to muck up the moon but they can't heat a flat. If they were smart they'd invent a robot who would fetch me a juice whenever I wanted, and take care of the housework without me having to be nice and listen to them droning on.

Mariette won't be coming tomorrow, all well and good I'm bored stiff with her old dad and his cancer. Anyway I've got her broken in, she knows her place more or less. Some of them slap rubber gloves on to do the washing up and act like the lady of the house; I wouldn't put up with that. On the other hand you don't want sluts who leave hairs in the salad and fingermarks on the doors. Tristan's a prat. I was very good with the help. I just wish they'd get on with it without all the drama. You have to train them properly just as you have to train children to turn them into proper people.

Tristan hasn't trained Francis, rotten old Mariette's left me in the lurch, the room will be a pigsty after they've been. They'll arrive with a fancy present, kisses all round I'll serve little cakes and Francis will trot out the answers his father's drummed into him, he already lies like a grown-up. I must talk to Tristan about him; it's always bad when a child's deprived of his mother, he turns into a hooligan or a nancy, you don't want that. Why am I being so bloody reasonable when my heart is breaking? All I want to do is yell, 'It's UNNATURAL to take a son away from his mother'.

'Threaten him with divorce' Dédé said. He just laughed. Men gang up on you and the law's so unfair and Tristan's got so much clout that I'll get all the blame. He'd get custody not a penny more for me and I'd lose the flat, as well. It's blackmail and I can't do a thing about it. An allowance and the flat in exchange for Francis. I am at his mercy. You can't defend yourself with no money you are less than nothing, double zero. What a clot I've been, I let all that money slip through my fingers, unselfish twit. I should have made the suckers dig deep in their pockets. If I had stayed with Florent I'd have got myself a lovely little nest-egg. But Tristan was mad about me, I took pity on him, and look what happened. The dope walked out on me just because I wouldn't grovel at his feet and treat him like some kind of Napoleon.

I'll show him. Tell him I'm going to tell the little one the truth; 'I'm not sick, I'm not sick. I only live alone because your swine of a father let me down; he sweet-talked me then he tortured me and then he practically beat me up'. Have hysterics in front of the little one, cut my wrists on their doorstep, something like that. I've got plenty of ammunition I'll use it then he'll come back to me, I won't have to be alone in this dump with those people upstairs trampling all over me and the radio next door getting me up every morning and no one to bring me a snack when I'm hungry. I can't bear it. Two weeks now the plumber has been fobbing me off when it's a woman alone they tell themselves anything will do men are such a let down when you're down they walk all over you. I show my teeth I hold my head up but they spit on a woman alone.

The porter's got a dirty laugh 'playing the radio at 10 in the morning is within the statutory regulations' as if he really thought he could put me down with fancy words. But I got my own back, four nights running on the phone, they knew it was me but they couldn't prove it. I laughed and laughed.

A man under my roof. The plumber will come, the porter will greet me politely, the neighbours will put a sock in it. Fuck it. I want some dignity I want my husband my son my own front door just like everyone else.

COMMENTARY: Murielle is a mass of discomfort and irritation. She's lived alone and the effects are showing. She literally sits there and stews in her own anger. This is not a self-pitying speech but one where all the blame is placed elsewhere. Murielle is full of spite and vengeance which make for a lively delivery of the monologue. The speech is full revenge scenarios. One of her main preoccupations is security: property and money are mentioned over and over. This is an important issue. Children are also a preoccupation but the child she mentions, Francis, also sounds like a piece of property. No mention is made in this speech of the daughter who committed suicide. The topic here is men and their injustice towards women.

The Woman Who Cooked Her Husband
Debbie Isitt

Scene 5. Somewhere near Liverpool, England.

Hilary (40s) is married to Kenneth, an aging Teddy boy. 'She is dressed in a green taffeta outfit, green tights and shoes. She wears her hair in a beehive.' She is an expert cook and homemaker. After nineteen years of marriage, Kenneth starts to have an affair with another woman. Hilary is bitter and resentful that her years of trying to be a good wife have got her nowhere. In this speech she reflects on her lot.

HILARY. Hilary – once married to Kenneth – once attractive vivacious – virile – Hilary – once wife – woman of the world – of the home – the home being the world – Hilary – ex-wife – divorcee – dishevelled – dishonourable – Hilary – how are you? You're looking well! Hilary – are you sleeping at night – poor cow – Hilary, how is he – do you ever see him? – Hilary what of her – how can you stand it? Hilary where did you go wrong – Hilary – it wasn't your fault – Hilary come out with us – Hilary can I get you anything? – Hilary pull yourself together – oh Hilary – not crying again – Hilary he'll be back – Hilary forget him – Hilary men they're all the same Hilary Hilary Hilary! When are you going to wake up – you're not the girl you were – saw Ken today he's looking younger – getting on with his life – I hear they're getting married – will you go – what you need is another fella – someone to cheer you up – come on Hilary give it a rest – it's all been over a long time ago – can't you think of anything else – piss off Hilary you're boring us to tears, you're not the only one you know – so it was nineteen years – it's in the past – look to the future – Hilary for God's sake he's not coming back – and if he did – would you want him now? He's not coming back – he's not coming back.

COMMENTARY: At a critical moment when her husband has just left her, Hilary tries to find an identity she can cling to. She keeps invoking her own name. But she's shattered. All the voices in her head intrude on her at once, coming from every direction: a cacophony of clichés from family and well-meaning friends. Time speeds along into the future and still the shock and guilt of the break-up fester. Kenneth's not coming back and she knows it. The speech is totally devoid of false hope and optimism. It also plants the seeds for her later revenge. Eventually she cooks and eats her husband.

─────────

Laura (20s-30s) starts as Kenneth's mistress, the other woman. (See also Decadence *and* To *for contrasting speeches.) She wears the same clothes as Hilary but is younger and sexier. She has been with Kenneth for several years and has finally persuaded him to leave his wife and marry her. Laura hates being tied down to a house but likes to go out and have fun. Here she and Kenneth are squabbling as they get ready to go out to Hilary's for a dinner party.*

LAURA. I don't like being a woman – I don't like it!!! I don't like being banished to the kitchen at parties talking about stupid things with stupid females – I want to be where you are with the men all laughing and joking and drinking and smoking – I want to join in! I can't do the things you ask of me – I'm not like your other wife – I'm not cut out for household chores – I cannot stand the monotonous, endless routines, the mindless activitites involved – who gives a fuck if the door knobs aren't polished?! Why make the bed, just to sleep in it again – I can't see the point – it doesn't make sense! You do it if you want to – hire someone – hire Hilary – anything just to get the pressure off my back. I do my best for you don't I? It's not like I'm lazy or stupid or incompetent – I starve myself for you – I try and get my fat bum down and my small tits up – I exercise! I know I'm no great cordon bleu chef but I have a go – the thanks I get. Have you any idea what it feels like to drool

120

over cookbooks all day, fantasizing about delicious recipes that I'm not allowed to eat in case I get fat and even if I could eat them I couldn't fucking cook them for the life of me because I'm so crap! What happened to me? I was young and sexy – you wanted me – now I'm a nervous wreck – what have I done – where have I gone wrong?

COMMENTARY: The relationship between Laura and Kenneth is none too cosy and it has radically deteriorated with time. Kenneth compares Laura once too often to Hilary his wife which she resents. He is always complaining that she doesn't cook and that she is starving him to death, whereas Hilary was an excellent cook. But Laura has no intention of being a domestic slave. She enjoys being a different sort of woman from Kenneth's wife Hilary. She wants to be treated as Kenneth's equal and lets him know this in no uncertain terms. The fact that they are going to dinner at Kenneth's former home with his wife must be adding to the tension and explosive atmosphere.

Women Laughing
Michael Wall

Act 2. The garden of a mental institution in North London.

Maddy Catchpole (20s-30s) is a suburban housewife. She is married to Tony who is a patient at a mental institution. He has had a complete breakdown and is doped into docility. His problems all came to a head when he and Maddy were visiting Colin and Stephanie. While the men were sitting in the garden making small talk the women were inside preparing a salad. The men's conversation was repeatedly interrupted by laughter from the kitchen which irritated them. The women were laughing at the coincidence that both of their husbands were in psychotherapy. Their menacing laughter proved to be the final straw for Tony and it pushed him over the edge as he confessed to an overwhelming desire to kill Maddy. The calm of their banal suburban world was shattered irrevocably. By a coincidence it turns out that Colin is also a patient at the same institution. In this scene both Steph and Maddy are visiting their husbands but neither of them seem particularly distressed by their spouse's conditions. In this speech Maddy strives to analyze her situation.

MADDY. I suppose I should have *talked* to him more. That's what they always say, isn't it? Talk it over and get it out into the open, sort of thing? The trouble is, he's always been a lot cleverer than me. My mother always used to say, Never marry 'em cleverer than yourself. A bit difficult in my case. I mean I'd never have got married, would I?
[STEPH. Don't be silly.]
He's always used words I don't understand. I'd look them up and everything, but then I'd go and forget them. Whereas he – he'd look them up and straight away he'd be – peppering his conversation with them. He would, he'd pepper it. And I'd stop and say Eh, that's the word you didn't know yesterday

and had to look up! The looks he used to give me. Especially when it was somebody he was out to impress. Used to embarrass him something dreadful. (*She laughs.*) But it is a bit of a cheat, that, isn't it? Pretending you've always talked like that when you've only just learned what the word means.
[STEPH. Oh, I suppose so.]
You don't have to agree with me.
[STEPH. No, it's just that men don't like to be teased.
MADDY (*indignant*). Well, I know but] . . . I never did it in a nasty way.
[STEPH. No.]
I mean, did it sound nasty to you, the way I described it?
[STEPH. No, no.]
Because, I mean, you've got to keep your feet on the ground, haven't you? Everyone has.
[STEPH. Oh yes.]
It's all part of being married.

COMMENTARY: Maddy tends to speak before she thinks and is prone to wittering on in mindless clichés. Maddy protects herself from guilt and reality by constantly putting herself at a disadvantage: she's not as bright as her husband, doesn't understand what words mean, has never been nasty. Her marriage and her spouse are clearly in peril but Maddy plays the innocent who can't quite comprehend what is going on around her. Anytime her motives are questioned she reacts with hurt pride. She likes to talk in clichés in the hope they will deflect difficult questions: 'I mean, you've got to keep your feet on the ground, haven't you?' She's sounds shallow but she works very hard to ensure that guilt does not come her way. She looks at her husband as if he were a problem well outside herself.

Your Home in the West
Rod Wooden

Act 1. The living room of a first floor council flat in the West End of Newcastle upon Tyne. A Friday afternoon in late November 1987.

Jean Robson (mid-30s) is divorced from Micky and she has a new boyfriend, Sean. She met Micky when she was sixteen: 'He was the same as me, just hanging about the streets. I'd just been hoyed out by me ma, she reckoned I was after her fancy man.' The two of them set up as a team together working Elswick Road; she would proposition men and then he would rob them. When they divorced she went back to prostitution in Middlesborough: 'It was what I was good at, even Micky said.' She leads a hand-to-mouth existence on a council estate, endlessly trying to make ends meet. She and Micky have two children, fifteen-year-old Sharon and seven-year-old Michael who is a tearaway always truanting from school. In this scene Jean is reaching the end of her tether. Jean's mother-in-law, Jeannie, has been claiming that it was only thanks to her that Jean ended up with custody of the children instead of the violent and foul-mouthed Micky. Jean is also worried because Michael has done a bunk from school, injuring a kitchen helper as he escaped over the school wall. In this speech Jean turns her anger on Jeannie.

JEAN. Oh I know what I'm saying all right but. I don't doubt you wanted me to have the bairns. You knew you couldn't cope with them, and you knew Micky didn't want them, he was just trying it on to spite us. You're not daft, I'll give you that, not daft by a long chalk. (*Pause.*) But *I* wanted them. When I came back from Middlesborough I was all for turning over a new leaf. No more Micky. No more Elswick Road. Just me and the bairns. Heaven, it could have been, if only he'd left us alone. (*Pause.*) But he couldn't. Leastways he couldn't leave Michael alone. Always had to be interfering, stirring

124

him up. First it was just against me, and then when Sean came on the scene he was stirring him up against him as well. But clever. Dead clever, I'll give him that. (*Mimics.*) 'Want to come for a ride in my car down the coast, son? Sean hasn't got a car has he?' 'Don't worry your mam and Sean about that son, they haven't got as much money as me. We'll go down town in the car and I'll get you one.' (*Normal voice.*) Do you know what he bought him last week? A baseball bat. The bairn's seven year old, what does he want with a baseball bat? Nearly put some kid's eye out with it, till I took it away from him. (*Pause.*) Do you know what Michael calls him? Magic daddy. Magic daddy can do anything. Magic daddy's got a big car, magic daddy's got lots of money, magic daddy's the strongest man in Newcastle, why he can even climb up walls with his bare hands and get into bad people's houses and take all their money away from them. It's a wonder magic daddy can't friggin fly.

[JEANNIE. You can't blame a man for taking an interest in his own flesh and blood. Michael's his own flesh and blood after all.]

It's no use talking to you Jeannie. You're just like Micky, you've got an answer for friggin everything. Oh you'll moan on about him not giving you enough money and suchlike. But anything else and you think the sun shines out of his friggin backside. Always wiping his arse for him, so I suppose you've got to think that. Who did he run to when I'd had enough of him? Back to his mammy, back to his friggin wet nurse. Thirty-three year old and he's still living with his mother, paying no rent, getting all his meals, his washing done, bringing back little bits of lasses and knocking them off under her roof, and she says nowt. Never has said nowt, always let him have whatever he wants. Couldn't keep the father could you Jeannie, so you thought you'd have the son instead. Have a son and man all rolled into one. Well you got what you wanted. And I hope you friggin choke on it.

COMMENTARY: Jean speaks bluntly and directly to Jeannie; nothing is hidden, no feelings are spared. She talks about a man who clearly has a hold over other women, his son and his mother Jeannie. There might be some jealousy in among her spite. So Jean has to work hard to puncture the illusion of this 'magic' man. Unfortunately she cannot point to anything specific to up-end the image of Micky, except that he now lives at home. Part of Micky's charm is his duplicity. He's one of life's great truants and he still hasn't been caught. His son Michael is following in his footsteps. But Jean's slate is not altogether clean either. Not the best of mothers herself, the irony is that Jean here is attacking Jeannie for being a bad parent.

Play Sources

After Easter by Anne Devlin (Faber)

Angels in America by Tony Kushner (Nick Hern Books)

Assassins by Stephen Sondheim and John Weidman (TCG/Nick Hern Books)

Belfry by Billy Roche in *The Wexford Trilogy* (Nick Hern Books)

Brontëburgers by Victoria Wood in *Up to You, Porky* (Mandarin)

Burn This by Lanford Wilson (Warner Chappell)

Can't Stand Up for Falling Down by Richard Cameron (Methuen)

Cigarettes and Chocolate by Anthony Minghella in *Interior: Room Exterior: City* (Methuen)

The Conquest of the South Pole by Manfred Karge (Methuen)

Death and the Maiden by Ariel Dorfman (Nick Hern Books)

Decadence by Steven Berkoff in *Steven Berkoff Collected Plays: Volume II* (Faber)

Digging for Fire by Declan Hughes (Methuen)

Etta Jenks by Marlane Meyer (Methuen)

The Fastest Clock in the Universe by Philip Ridley (Methuen)

Frankie and Johnny in the Clair de Lune by Terrence McNally (Warner Chappell)

Giving Notes by Victoria Wood in *Up to You, Porky* (Mandarin)

Her Aching Heart by Bryony Lavery (Methuen)

Here by Michael Frayn (Methuen)

Hush by April de Angelis in *Frontline Intelligence I* (Methuen)

The Last Yankee by Arthur Miller (Methuen)

Laughing Wild by Christopher Durang (Samuel French)

Lettice and Lovage by Peter Shaffer (Penguin)

The Love Space Demands by Ntozake Shange in *Shange Plays: One* (Methuen)

Low Level Panic by Claire McIntyre in *First Run* (Nick Hern Books)

The Madness of Esme and Shaz by Sarah Daniels in *Daniels Plays: One* (Methuen)

Man to Man by Manfred Karge in *The Conquest of the South Pole* (Methuen)

Molly Sweeney by Brian Friel (Penguin)

Moonlight by Harold Pinter (Faber)

My Mother Said I Never Should by Charlotte Keatley (Methuen)

Oleanna by David Mamet (Methuen)

The Pitchfork Disney by Philip Ridley (Methuen)

The Ride Down Mount Morgan by Arthur Miller (Methuen)

The Rise and Fall of Little Voice by Jim Cartwright (Methuen)

Serious Money by Caryl Churchill (Methuen)

Shades by Sharman Macdonald (Faber)

The Sisters Rosensweig by Wendy Wasserstein (Harcourt Brace)

Six Degrees of Separation by John Guare (Methuen)

Some Americans Abroad by Richard Nelson (Faber)

Talking Heads by Alan Bennett (BBC Books)

Talking in Tongues by Winsome Pinnock in *Black Plays: Three* (Methuen)

Ten Tiny Fingers, Nine Tiny Toes by Sue Townsend (Methuen)

Three Birds Alighting on a Field by Timberlake Wertenbaker (Faber)

Three Hotels by Jon Robin Baitz (Dramatists Play Service)

To by Jim Cartwright (Methuen)

The Woman Destroyed by Simone de Beauvoir in *Plays by Women: Ten* (Methuen)

The Woman Who Cooked her Husband by Debbie Isitt (Warner Chappell)

Women Laughing by Michael Wall (Micheline Steinberg, Playwrights' Agent, 110 Frognal, London NW3 6XU)

Your Home in the West by Rod Wooden (Methuen)

Acknowledgements

The editors and publishers gratefully acknowledge permission to reproduce copyright material in this book:

Jon Robin Baitz: *Three Hotels*. Copyright © 1992, 1993 by Available Light Productions, Inc. Reprinted by permission of the author's agent, William Morris Agency, 1350 Avenue of the Americas, New York, NY 10019, USA. Alan Bennett: from *Talking Heads*. Copyright © 1988 by Forelake Ltd. Reprinted by permission of BBC Books. Steven Berkoff: from *Decadence*. Copyright © 1981, 1982, 1983, 1986, 1989 by Steven Berkoff. Reprinted by permission of Faber and Faber Ltd. Richard Cameron: from *Can't Stand Up For Falling Down*. Copyright © 1991 by Richard Cameron. Reprinted by permission of Methuen London. Jim Cartwright: from *To*. Copyright © 1991 by Jim Cartwright. From *The Rise and Fall of Little Voice*. Copyright © 1992 by Jim Cartwright. Reprinted by permission of Methuen London. Caryl Churchill: from *Serious Money*. Copyright © 1987 by Caryl Churchill. Reprinted by permission of Methuen London. Sarah Daniels: from *The Madness of Esme and Shaz*. Copyright © 1994 by Sarah Daniels. Reprinted by permission of Methuen London. April de Angelis: from *Hush*. Copyright © 1992, 1993, by April de Angelis. Reprinted by permission of Methuen London. Simone de Beauvoir: from *The Woman Destroyed*. Adaptation copyright © 1991 by Diana Quick. Reprinted by permission of Methuen London. Anne Devlin: from *After Easter*. Copyright © 1994 by Anne Devlin. Reprinted by permission of Faber and Faber Ltd. Ariel Dorfman: from *Death and the Maiden*. Copyright © 1990 by Ariel Dorfman. Reprinted by permission of Nick Hern Books. Christopher Durang: from *Laughing Wild*. Copyright © 1988 by Christopher Durang. Reprinted by permission of the author's agent Helen Merrill, 435 West 23 Street #1A, New York, NY 10011, USA. Michael Frayn: from *Here*. Copyright © 1993 by Michael Frayn. Reprinted by permission of Methuen London. Brian Friel: from *Molly Sweeney*. Copyright © 1994 by Brian

Methuen Audition Books and Monologues

Methuen Modern Plays
include work by

Jean Anouilh
John Arden
Margaretta D'Arcy
Peter Barnes
Sebastian Barry
Brendan Behan
Edward Bond
Bertolt Brecht
Howard Brenton
Simon Burke
Jim Cartwright
Caryl Churchill
Noël Coward
Lucinda Coxon
Sarah Daniels
Nick Dear
Shelagh Delaney
David Edgar
David Eldridge
Dario Fo
Michael Frayn
John Godber
Paul Godfrey
David Greig
John Guare
Peter Handke
David Harrower
Jonathan Harvey
Iain Heggie
Declan Hughes
Terry Johnson
Sarah Kane
Charlotte Keatley
Barrie Keeffe
Howard Korder
Robert Lepage

Stephen Lowe
Doug Lucie
Martin McDonagh
John McGrath
Terrence McNally
David Mamet
Patrick Marber
Arthur Miller
Mtwa, Ngema & Simon
Tom Murphy
Phyllis Nagy
Peter Nichols
Joseph O'Connor
Joe Orton
Louise Page
Joe Penhall
Luigi Pirandello
Stephen Poliakoff
Franca Rame
Mark Ravenhill
Philip Ridley
Reginald Rose
David Rudkin
Willy Russell
Jean-Paul Sartre
Sam Shepard
Wole Soyinka
Shelagh Stephenson
C. P. Taylor
Theatre de Complicite
Theatre Workshop
Sue Townsend
Judy Upton
Timberlake Wertenbaker
Victoria Wood

Methuen Student Editions